CW01476395

HANDWRITING WORKBOOK FOR KIDS - BEGINNER WRITING

by

Smiling Toddlers Press

Powered by

Puzzle World University

Smiling Toddlers Press

Free Download
Activity Bonus, ready to print!

A kind request:
We are a young publishing company and would be grateful if you could leave a review Amazon with photos.

Thank you very much, have fun!

This book belongs to :

....

CAPITAL LETTERS IN CURSIVE

A B C D E F G

H I J K L M N

O P Q R S T U

V W X Y Z

NOTE: Trace over the dotted letters on the following pages then try writing the letters on your own in the blank space areas.

There are additional blank lined pages at the end of this workbook for more practice time.

lowercase letters in cursive

a b c d e f g h

i j k l m n o

p q r s t u v

w x y z

A A A A A A A A A

A A A A

a a a a a a a a a a a

a a a a

B B B B B B B B B

B B B B

b b b b b b b b b b b

b b b b

C C C C C C C C C C

C C C C

c c c c c c c c c c c c c

c c c c

D D D D D D D D

D D D D

d d d d d d d d d d d

d d d d

Try practice writing this letter one at a time - E.

Now practice writing your letters one at a time - F.

So, let's practice writing this letter one at a time - G.

G

g

Next, let's practice writing this letter one at a time - H.

Now practice writing this letter one at a time - I.

Let's practice writing this letter one at a time - J.

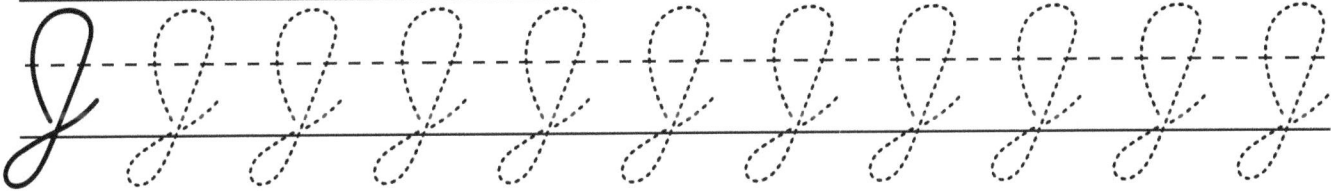

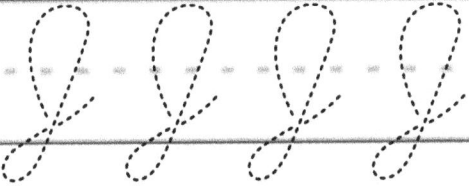

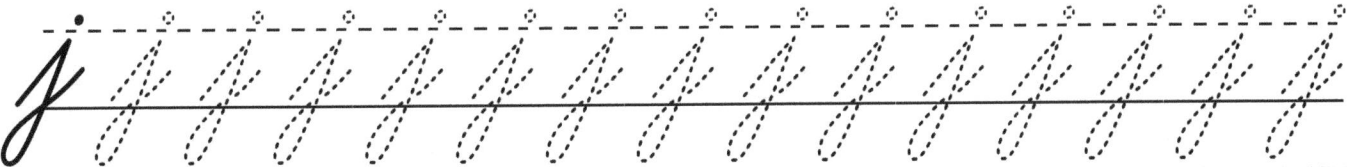

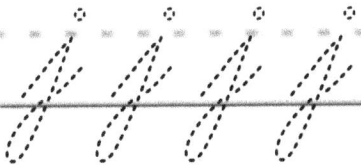

Try practice writing this letter one at a time - K.

Next, let's practice writing this letter one at a time - L.

L L L L L L L L L

L L L L

l l l l l l l l l l l l l

l l l l

Now practice writing this letter one at a time - M.

M M M M M M M

M M M M

m m m m m m m

m m m m

OK, try writing this letter one at a time - N.

Try practice writing this letter one at a time - O.

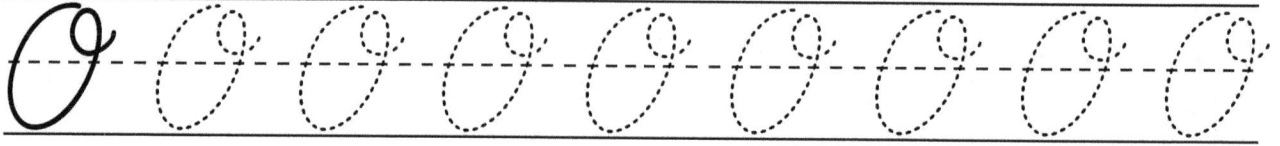

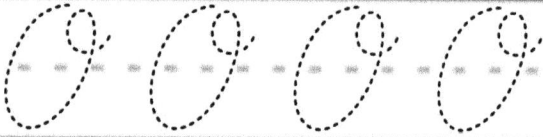

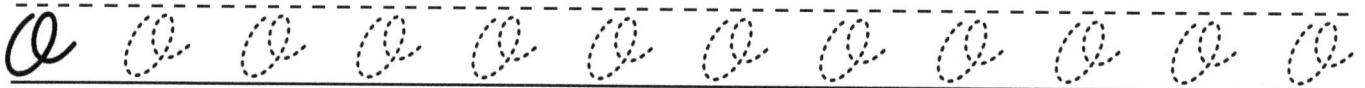

Next, let's practice writing this letter one at a time - P.

P

p

OK, try writing this letter one at a time - Q.

Now let’s practice writing this letter one at a time - R.

OK, now try writing this letter one at a time - S.

Next, let's practice writing this letter one at a time - T.

Now try writing this letter one at a time - U.

Try practice writing this letter one at a time - V.

Next, let’s practice writing this letter one at a time - W.

OK, try writing this letter one at a time - X.

First, let's practice writing this letter one at a time - Y.

OK, try writing this letter one at a time - Z.

CAPITAL LETTERS IN CURSIVE

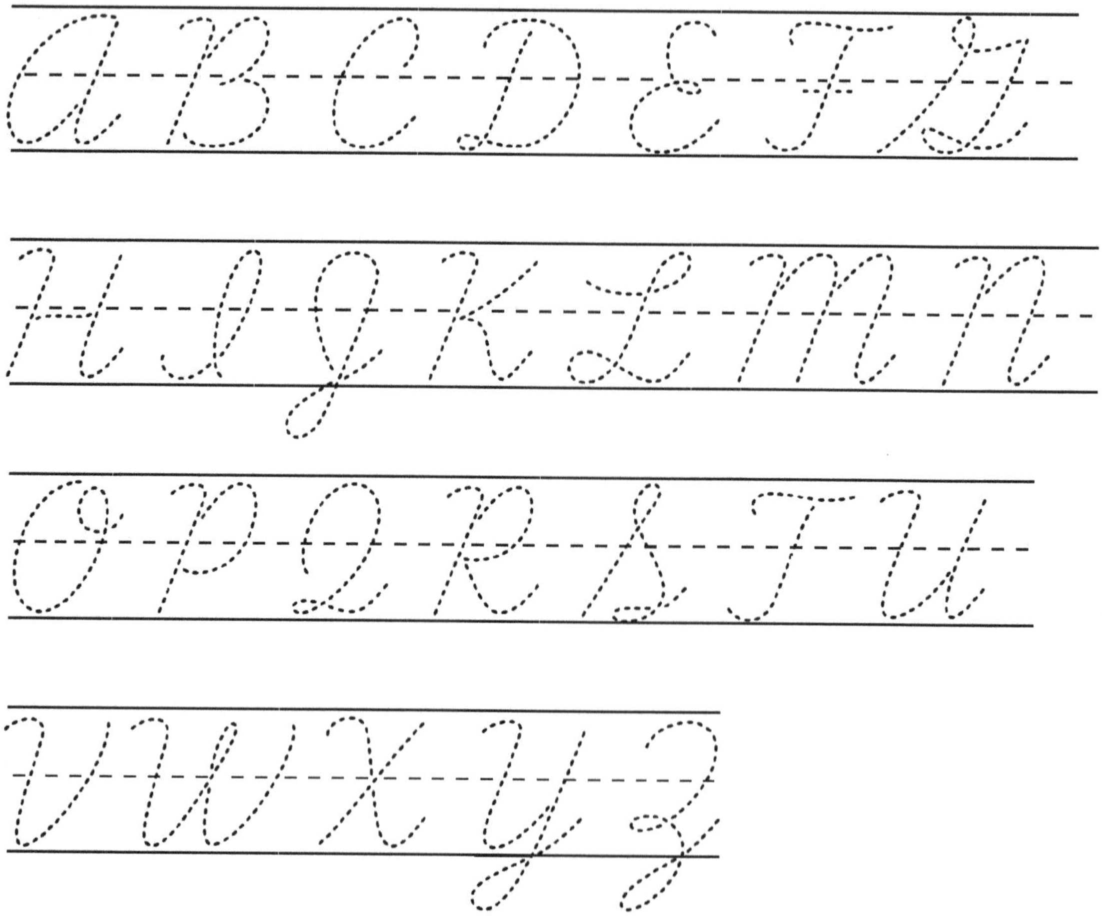

NOTE: Trace over the dotted letters on the following pages then try writing the letters on your own in the blank space areas.

There are additional blank lined pages at the end of this workbook for more practice time.

lowercase letters in cursive

a b c d e f g h

i j k l m n o

p q r s t u v

w x y z

Try writing these words one at a time.

Apple Apple Apple

Apple Apple Apple

apple apple apple

apple apple apple

Try writing these words one at a time.

Bear Bear Bear Bear

Bear Bear Bear

bear bear bear bear

bear bear bear

Try writing these words one at a time.

Cat Cat Cat Cat Cat

Cat Cat Cat

cat cat cat cat cat cat

cat cat cat cat

Try writing these words one at a time. 

Dog Dog Dog Dog Dog

Dog Dog Dog

dog dog dog dog dog

dog dog dog

Try writing these words one at a time.

Goat Goat Goat Goat

Goat Goat Goat

goat goat goat goat

goat goat goat

Try writing these words one at a time.

House House House

House House House

house house house

house house house

Try writing these words one at a time.

Igloo Igloo Igloo Igloo

Igloo Igloo Igloo

igloo igloo igloo igloo

igloo igloo igloo

Try writing these words one at a time.

Juice Juice Juice Juice

Juice Juice Juice

juice juice juice juice

juice juice juice

Try writing these words one at a time. 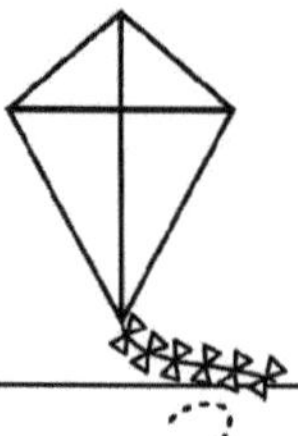

Kite Kite Kite Kite Kite

Kite Kite Kite

kite kite kite kite kite

kite kite kite

Try writing these words one at a time.

Lion Lion Lion Lion

Lion Lion Lion

lion lion lion lion

lion lion lion

Try writing these words one at a time.

Mouse Mouse Mouse

Mouse Mouse Mouse

mouse mouse mouse

mouse mouse mouse

Try writing these words one at a time. 

Nest Nest Nest Nest

Nest Nest Nest

nest nest nest nest

nest nest nest

Try writing these words one at a time.

Owl Owl Owl Owl

Owl Owl Owl

owl owl owl owl owl

owl owl owl

Try writing these words one at a time.

Plane Plane Plane

Plane Plane Plane

plane plane plane

plane plane plane

Try writing these words one at a time.

Quail Quail Quail

Quail Quail Quail

quail quail quail quail

quail quail quail

Try writing these words one at a time.

Rose Rose Rose Rose

Rose Rose Rose

rose rose rose rose rose

rose rose rose

Try writing these words one at a time.

Sun Sun Sun Sun

Sun Sun Sun

sun sun sun sun sun

sun sun sun

Try writing these words one at a time.

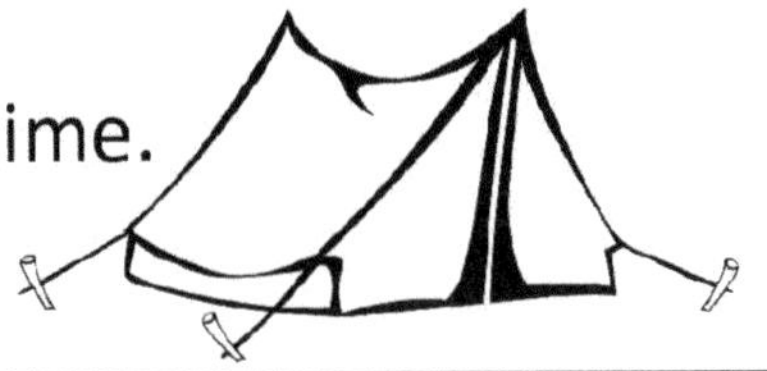

Tent *Tent Tent Tent*

Tent Tent Tent

tent *tent tent tent*

tent tent tent

Try writing these words one at a time.

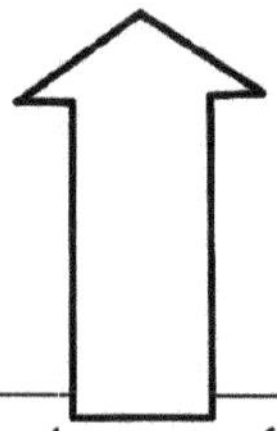

Up Up Up Up Up Up

Up Up Up

up up up up up up up

up up up

Try writing these words one at a time.

Van Van Van Van

Van Van Van

van van van van

van van van

Try writing these words one at a time.

Watch Watch Watch

Watch Watch

watch watch watch

watch watch watch

Try writing these words one at a time.

Xing Xing Xing Xing

Xing Xing

xing xing xing xing

xing xing xing

Try writing these words one at a time.

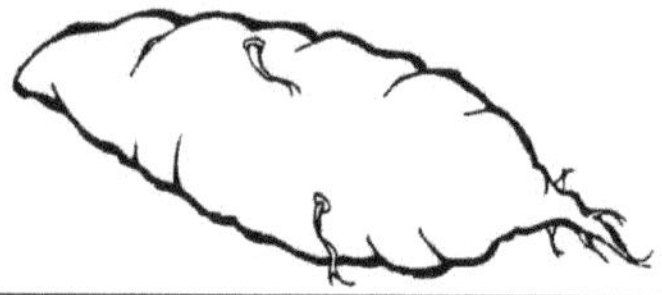

Yam Yam Yam Yam

Yam Yam Yam

yam yam yam yam

yam yam yam

Try writing these words one at a time.

Zebra Zebra Zebra

Zebra Zebra Zebra

zebra zebra zebra

zebra zebra zebra

CAPITAL LETTERS IN CURSIVE

A B C D E F G

H I J K L M N

O P Q R S T U

V W X Y Z

NOTE: Trace over the dotted letters on the following pages then try writing the letters on your own in the blank space areas.

There are additional blank lined pages at the end of this workbook for more practice time.

lowercase letters in cursive

a b c d e f g h

i j k l m n o

p q r s t u v

w x y z

First, let's practice writing a few sentences.

Apples taste good.

Apples taste good.

Apples are tasty.

Apples are tasty.

Now, let's practice writing a few sentences.

Boys like to play.

Boys like to play.

Boys love toys.

Boys love toys.

Try practice writing these sentences.

Cats meow.

Cats meow.

Cats purr.

Cats purr.

Now, let's practice writing these sentences.

Dogs bark.

Dogs bark.

Dogs dig.

Dogs dig.

First, let's practice writing a few sentences.

Eggs taste good.

Eggs taste good.

Eggs break.

Eggs break.

Now, let's practice writing these sentences.

Football is fun.

Football is fun.

Fly a kite.

Fly a kite.

Let's practice writing these sentences.

Go outside.

Go outside.

Giggle with me.

Giggle with me.

Try practice writing these sentences.

Hello friend.

Hello friend.

High in the sky.

High in the sky.

First, let's practice writing a few sentences.

Ice is cold.

Ice is cold.

Igloos are cool.

Igloos are cool.

Let's practice writing these sentences.

Jelly is good.

Jelly is good.

Jam is better.

Jam is better.

Now let's practice writing these sentences.

Kings rule.

Kings rule.

Keys open doors.

Keys open doors.

Try practice writing these sentences.

Leaves on trees.

Leaves on trees.

Lamps are bright.

Lamps are bright.

Let's practice writing these sentences.

Mice love cheese.

Mice love cheese.

Monsters are scary.

Monsters are scary.

Next, let's write these sentences.

Noses itch.

Noses itch.

Nicely done.

Nicely done.

Try practice writing these sentences.

Owls fly.

Owls fly.

Owls are birds.

Owls are birds.

Next, let's write these sentences.

Pandas are cute.

Pandas are cute.

Puppies are playful.

Puppies are playful.

Try writing these sentences next.

Questions are good.

Questions are good.

Quails are birds.

Quails are birds.

Try practice writing these sentences.

Roses smell good.

Roses smell good.

Red is pretty.

Red is pretty.

First, let's practice writing a few sentences.

School is cool.

School is cool.

Sun shines bright.

Sun shines bright.

Try writing these sentences next.

Toys are fun.

Toys are fun.

Tiny is cute.

Tiny is cute.

Now, let's practice writing these sentences.

Up there.

Up there.

Up and down.

Up and down.

Try practice writing these sentences.

Vans are cool.

Vans are cool.

Violas sound nice.

Violas sound nice.

First, let's practice writing a few sentences.

Watch me write.

Watch me write.

Write right.

Write right.

First, let's practice writing a few sentences.

Xenon is a gas.

Xenon is a gas.

X-rays work.

X-rays work.

First, let's practice writing a few sentences.

Yams are tasty.

Yams are tasty.

Yummy food.

Yummy food.

First, let's practice writing a few sentences.

Zip zap zit.

Zip zap zit.

Zoom or boom.

Zoom or boom.

Alphabet Coloring And Tracing

Aa *is for* Animals

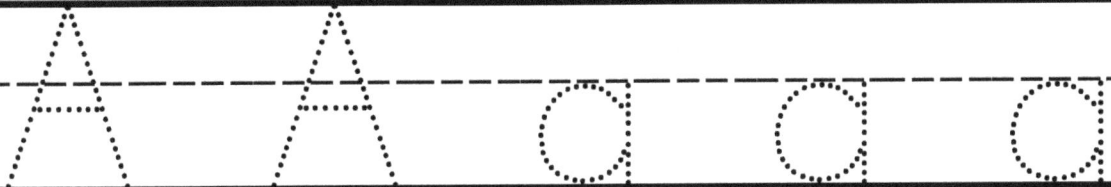

A A a a a

Bb *is for* Bat

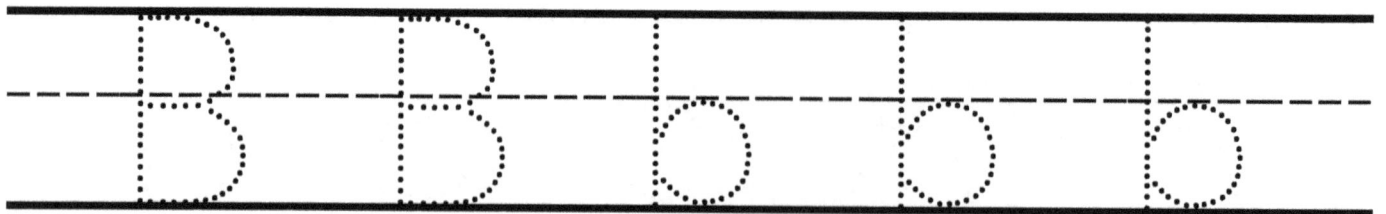

B B b b b

Cc is for Cow

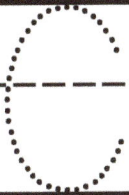

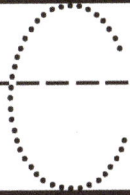

C C c c c

Dd *is for* Dolphin

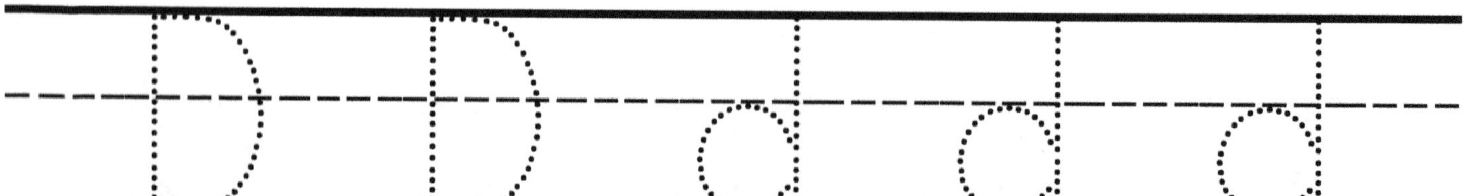

Ee is for Egg

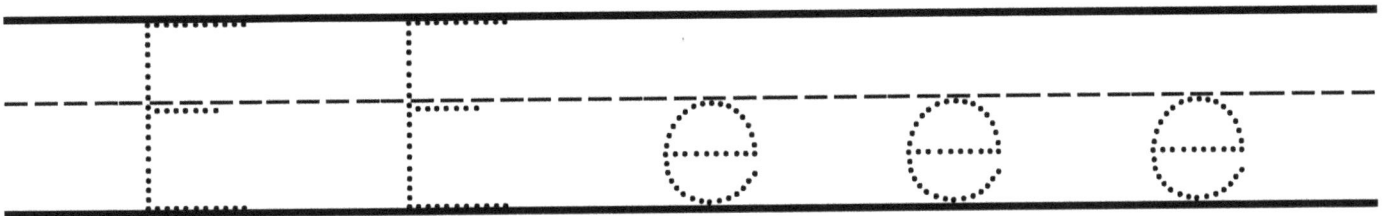

E E e e e

Ff *is for* Fish

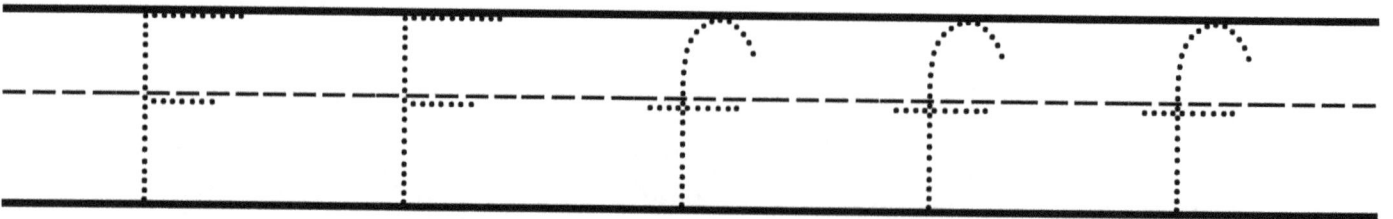

F F f f f

Gg is for Goat

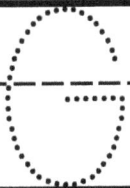

G G g g g

Hh *is for* Horse

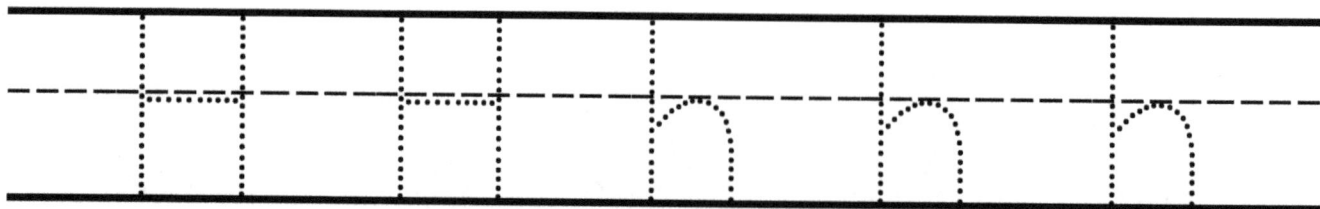

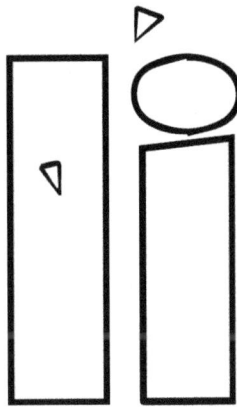

Ii *is for* Ice cream

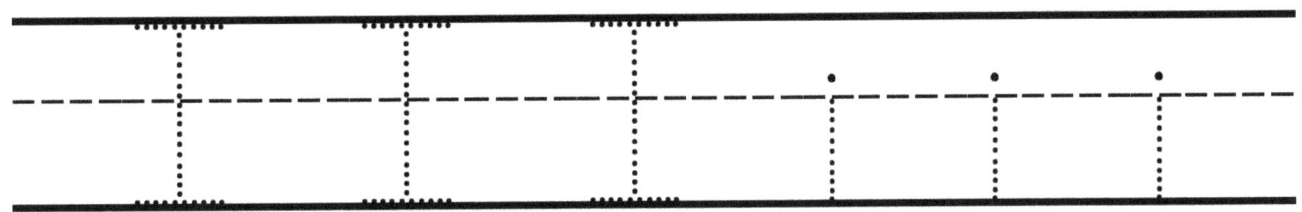

I I I i i i

Jj *is for* Jaguar

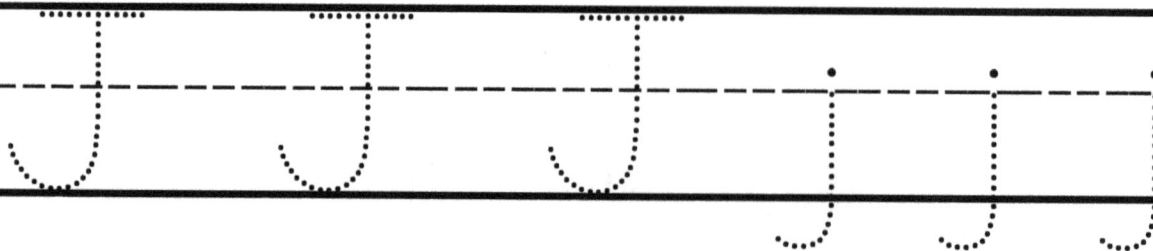

J J J j j j

Kk is for Kangaroo

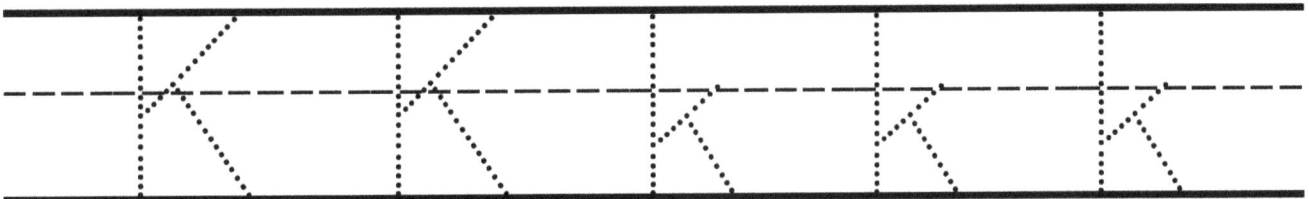

K K k k k

Ll is for Llama

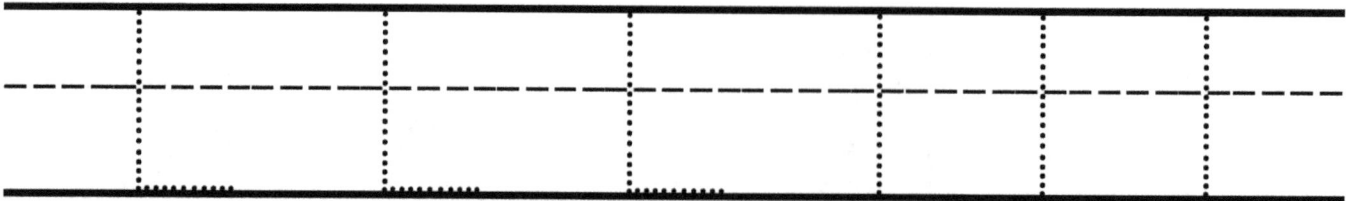

Mm *is for* Mouse

M M m m m

Nn *is for* Nest

N N n n n

O *is for* Orange

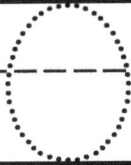

O O o o o

Pp

is for

Parrot

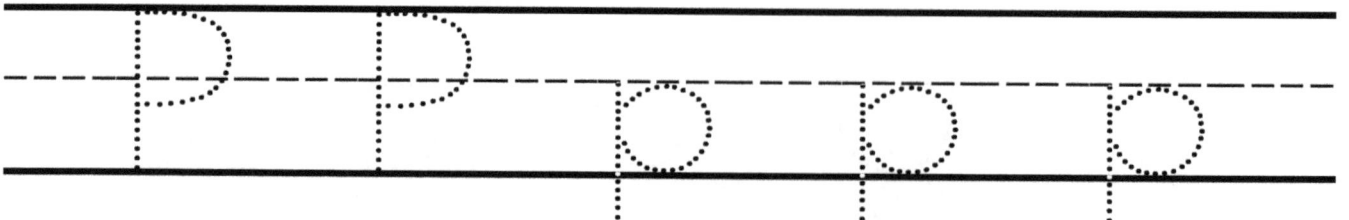

P P p p p

Qq is for Quail

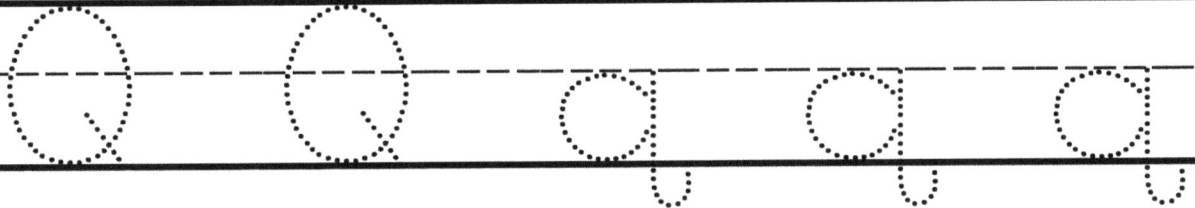

Q Q q q q

Rr is for Rabbit

R R r r r

S *is for* Spider

S S s s s

Tt *is for* Turtle

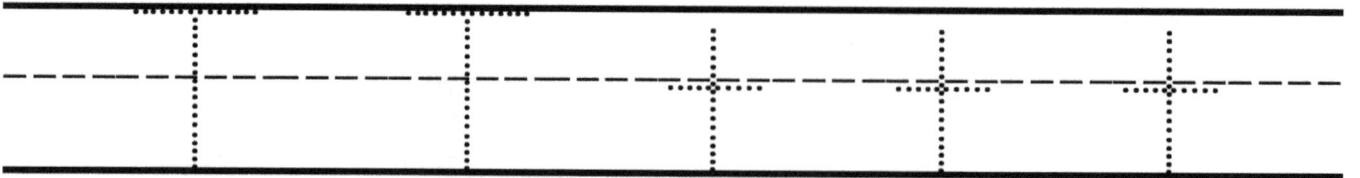

Uu is for Unicorn

V *is for* Vase

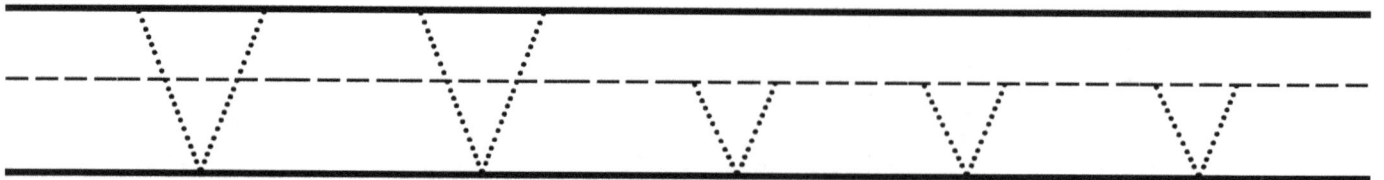

V V v v v

W *is for* Worm

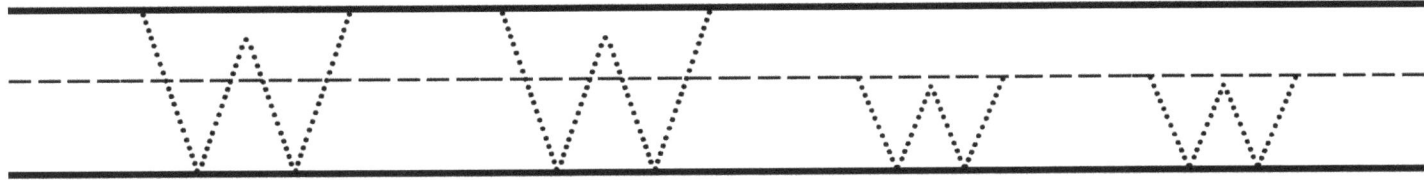

W W w w

X *is for* Xylophone

Yy *is for* Yak

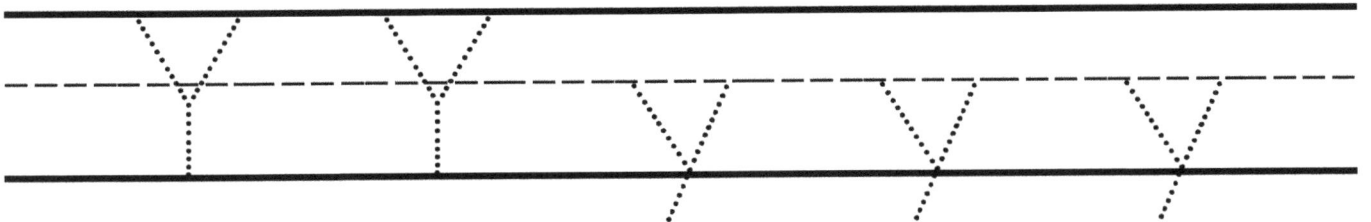

Y Y y y y

Z *is for* Zebra

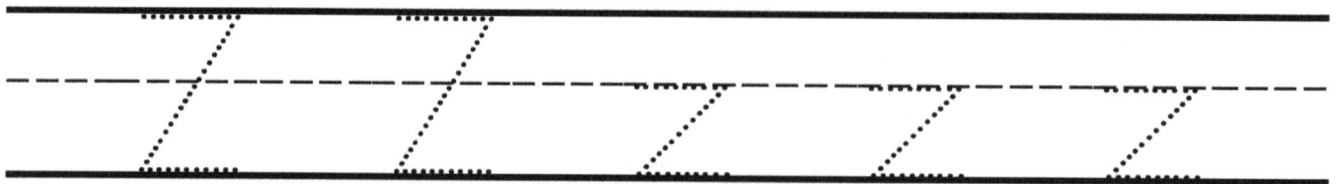

Alphabet Letter Tracing

Aa

apple

Aa

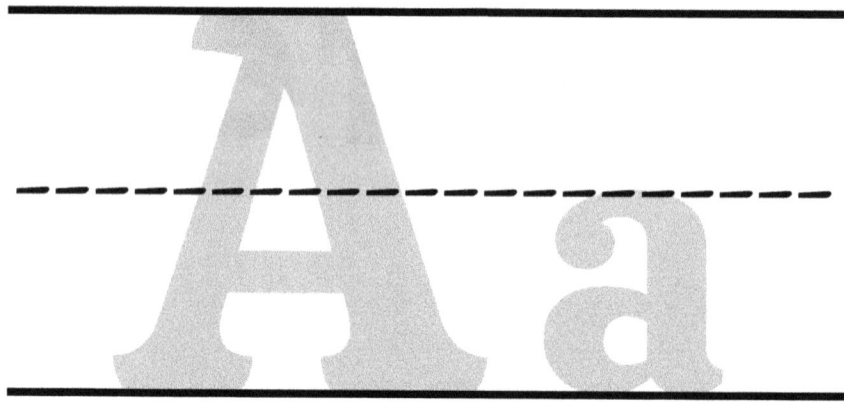

A is for Apple

A A A A A

A A A A A

A A A A A

A A A A A

A A A A A

A A A A A

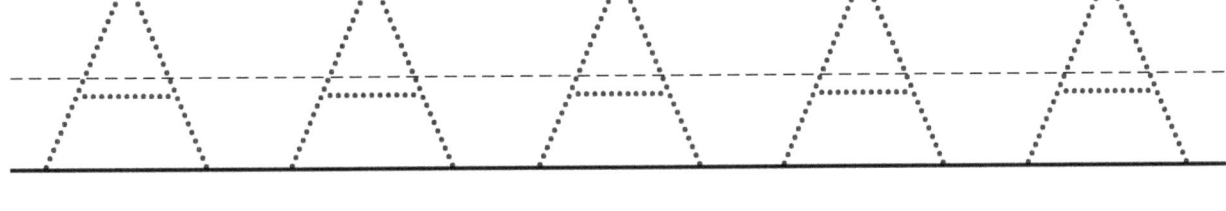

A A A A A

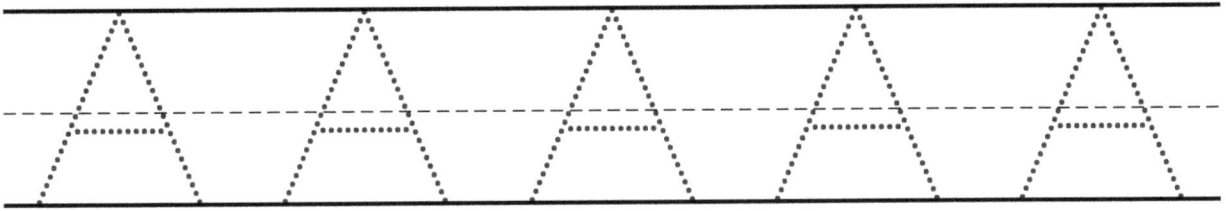

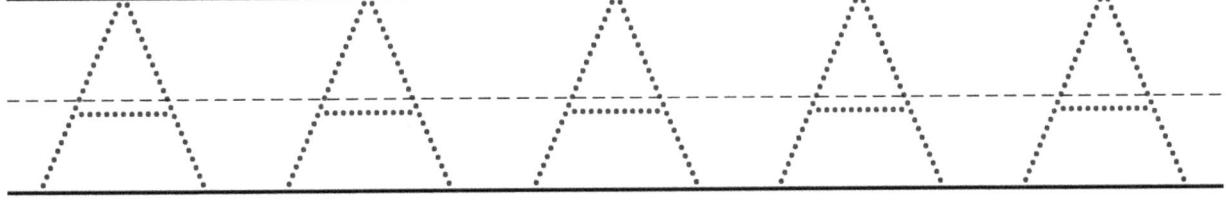

a a a a a a a a a

a a a a a a a a a

a a a a a a a a a

a a a a a a a a a

a a a a a a a a a

a a a a a a a a a

a a a a a a a a a

a a a a a a a a a

Bb

banana

Bb

B is for Banana

B B B B B

B B B B B

B B B B B

B B B B B

B B B B B

B B B B B

B B B B B

b b b b b

b b b b b

b b b b b

b b b b b

b b b b b

b b b b b

b b b b b

Cc

cat

C c

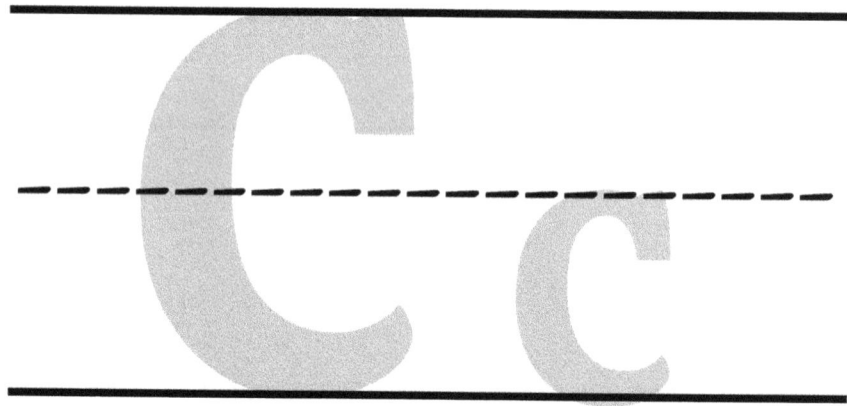

C is for Cat

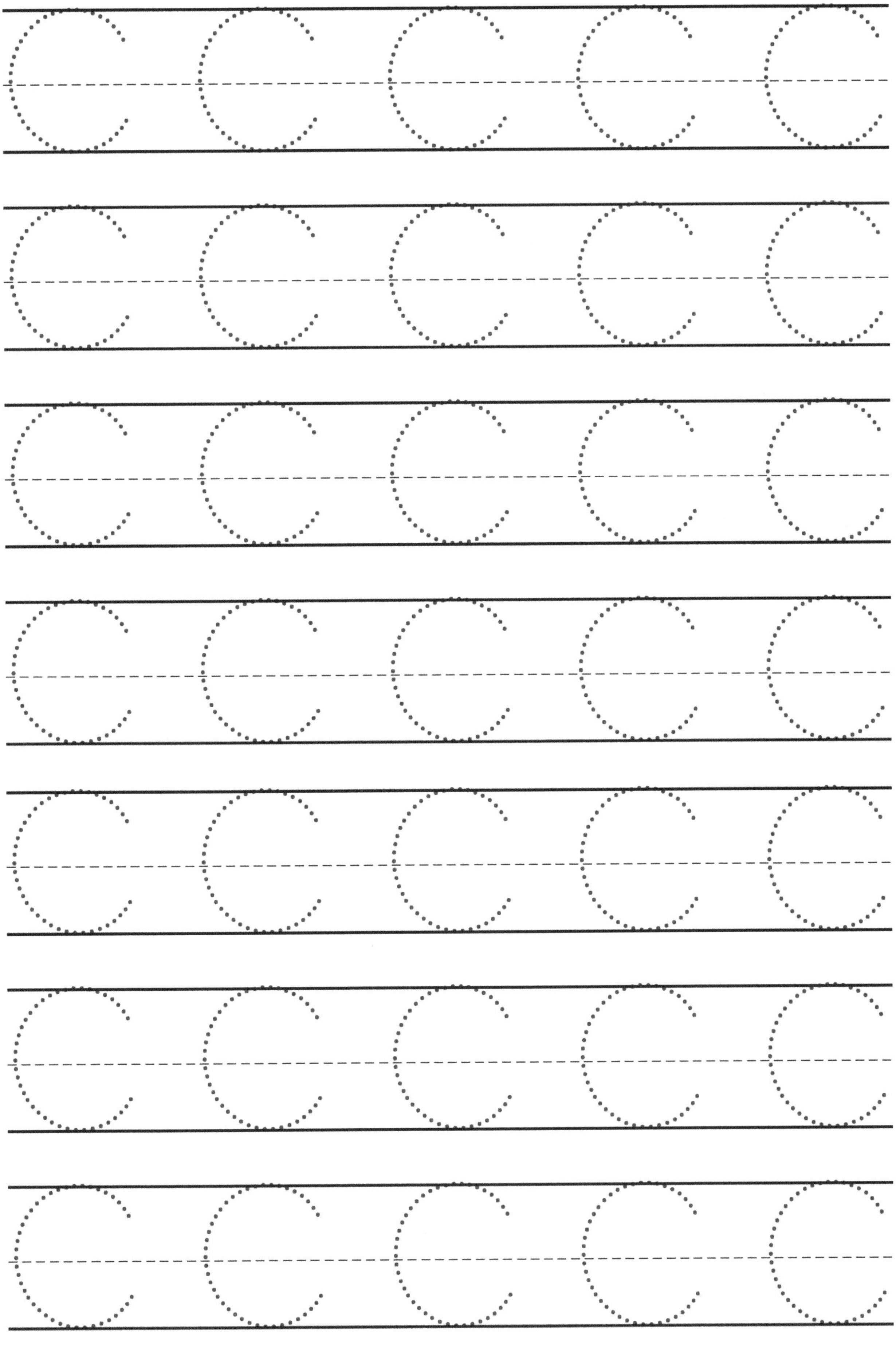

c c c c c c c c c

c c c c c c c c c

c c c c c c c c c

c c c c c c c c c

c c c c c c c c c

c c c c c c c c c

c c c c c c c c c

Dd

dinosaur

Dd

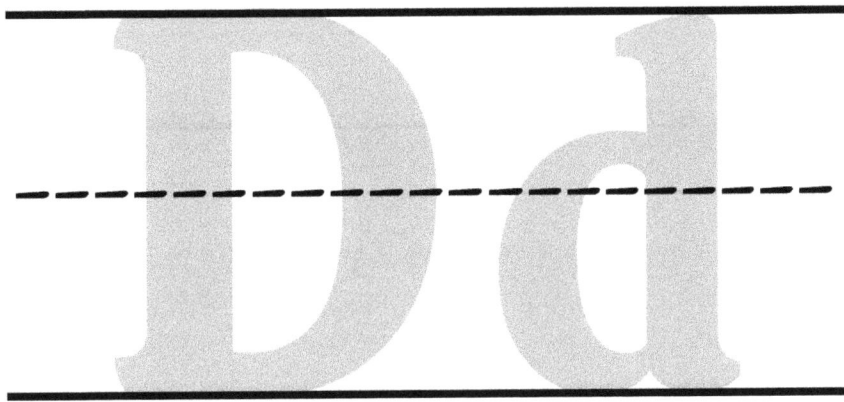

D is for Dinosaur

D D D D D

D D D D D

D D D D D

D D D D D

D D D D D

D D D D D

D D D D D

d d d d d d d d

d d d d d d d d

d d d d d d d d

d d d d d d d d

d d d d d d d d

d d d d d d d d

d d d d d d d d

d d d d d d d d

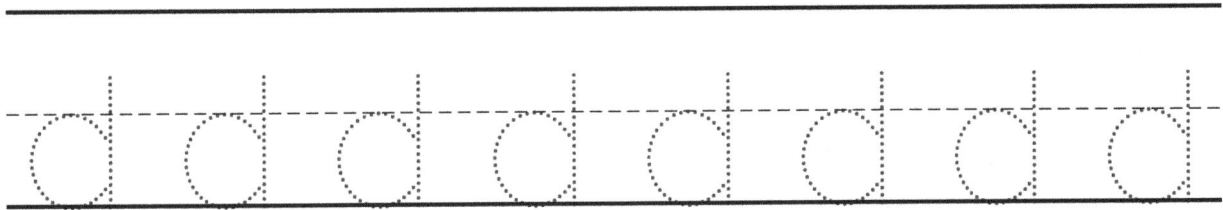

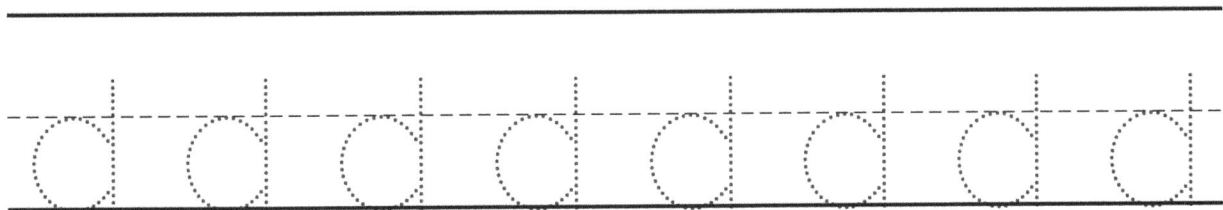

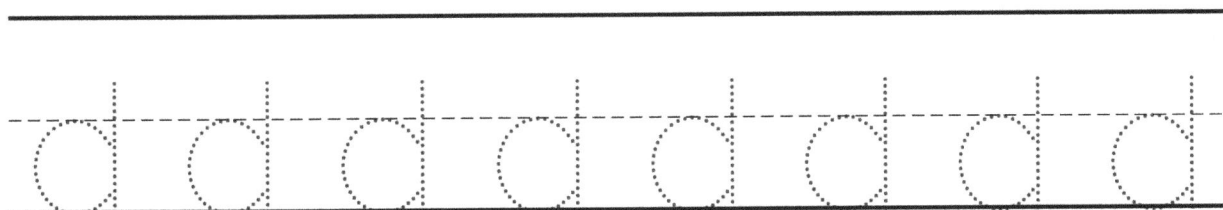

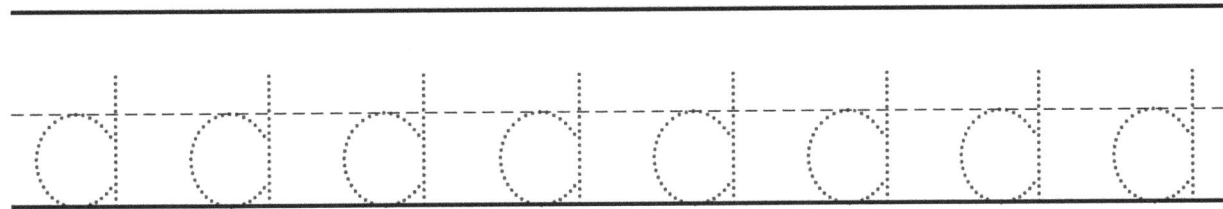

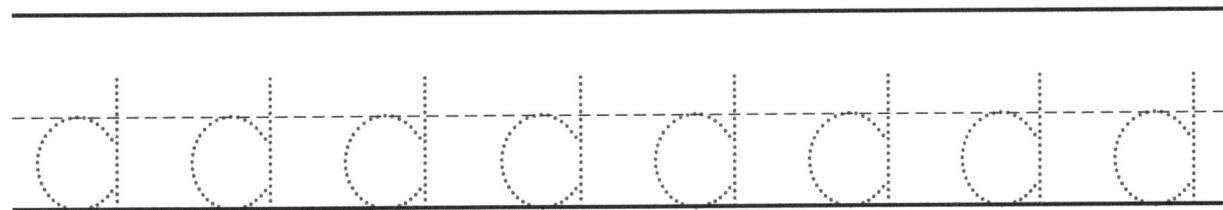

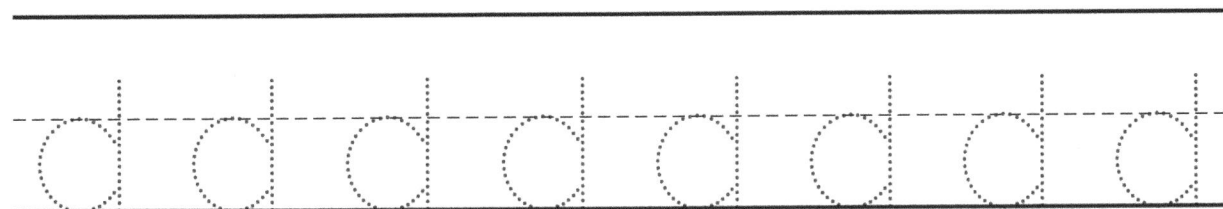

Ee

elephant

E e

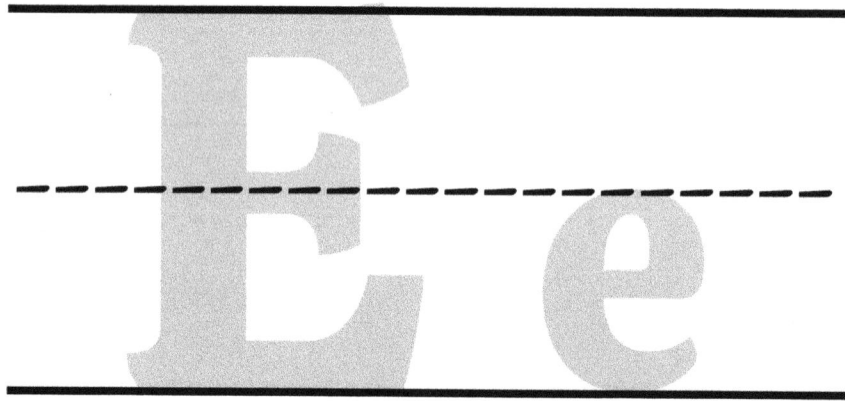

E is for Elephant

E E E E E

E E E E E

E E E E E

E E E E E

E E E E E

E E E E E

E E E E E

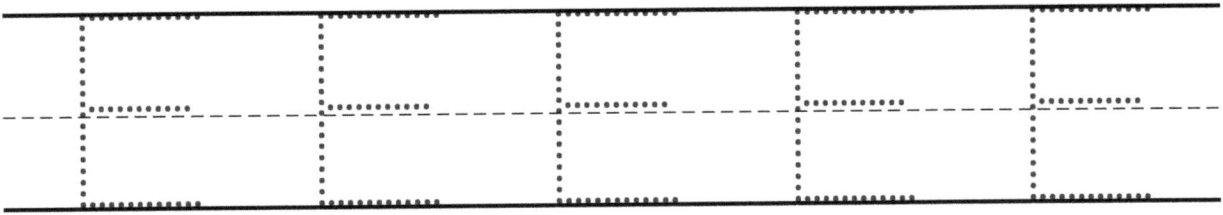

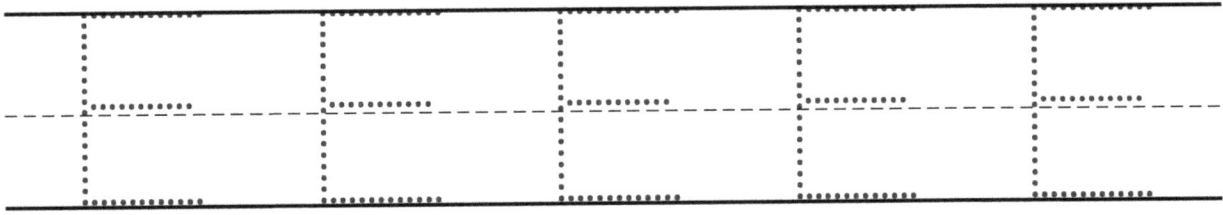

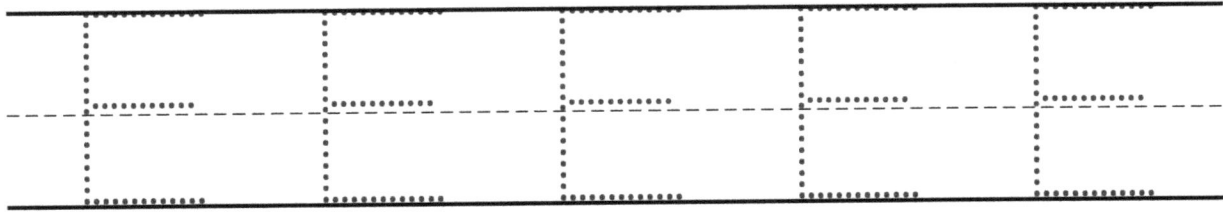

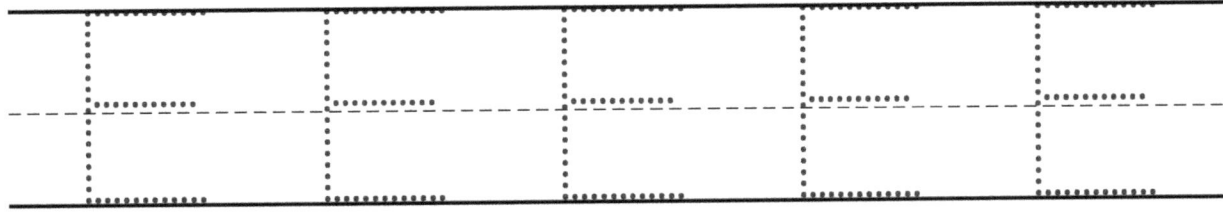

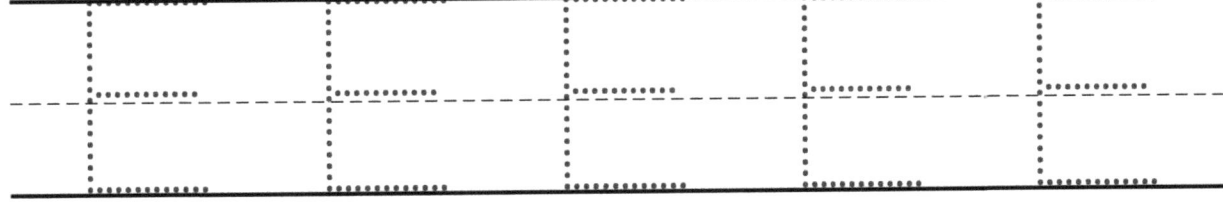

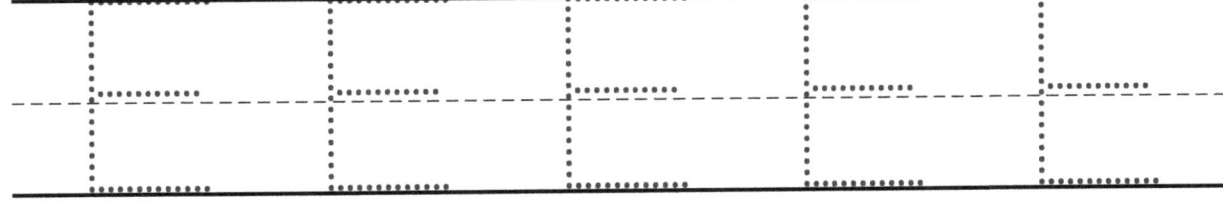

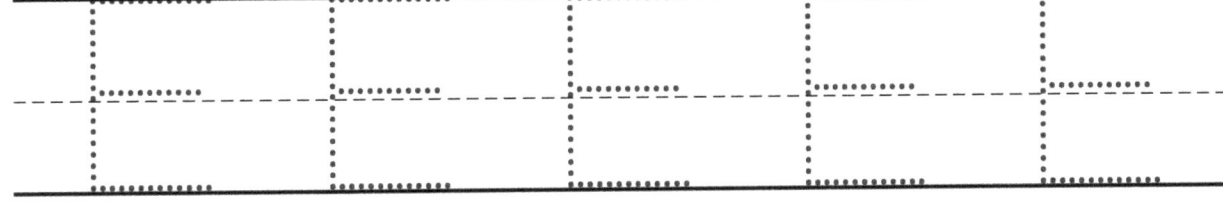

e e e e e e e e

e e e e e e e e

e e e e e e e e

e e e e e e e e

e e e e e e e e

e e e e e e e e

e e e e e e e e

Ff

fish

Ff

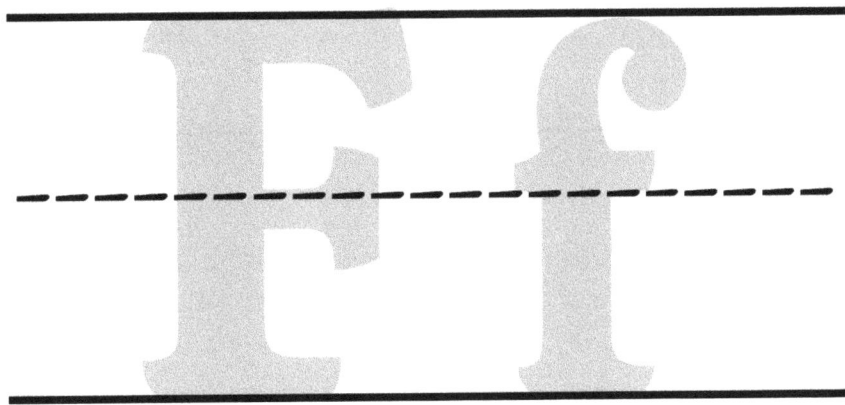

F is for Fish

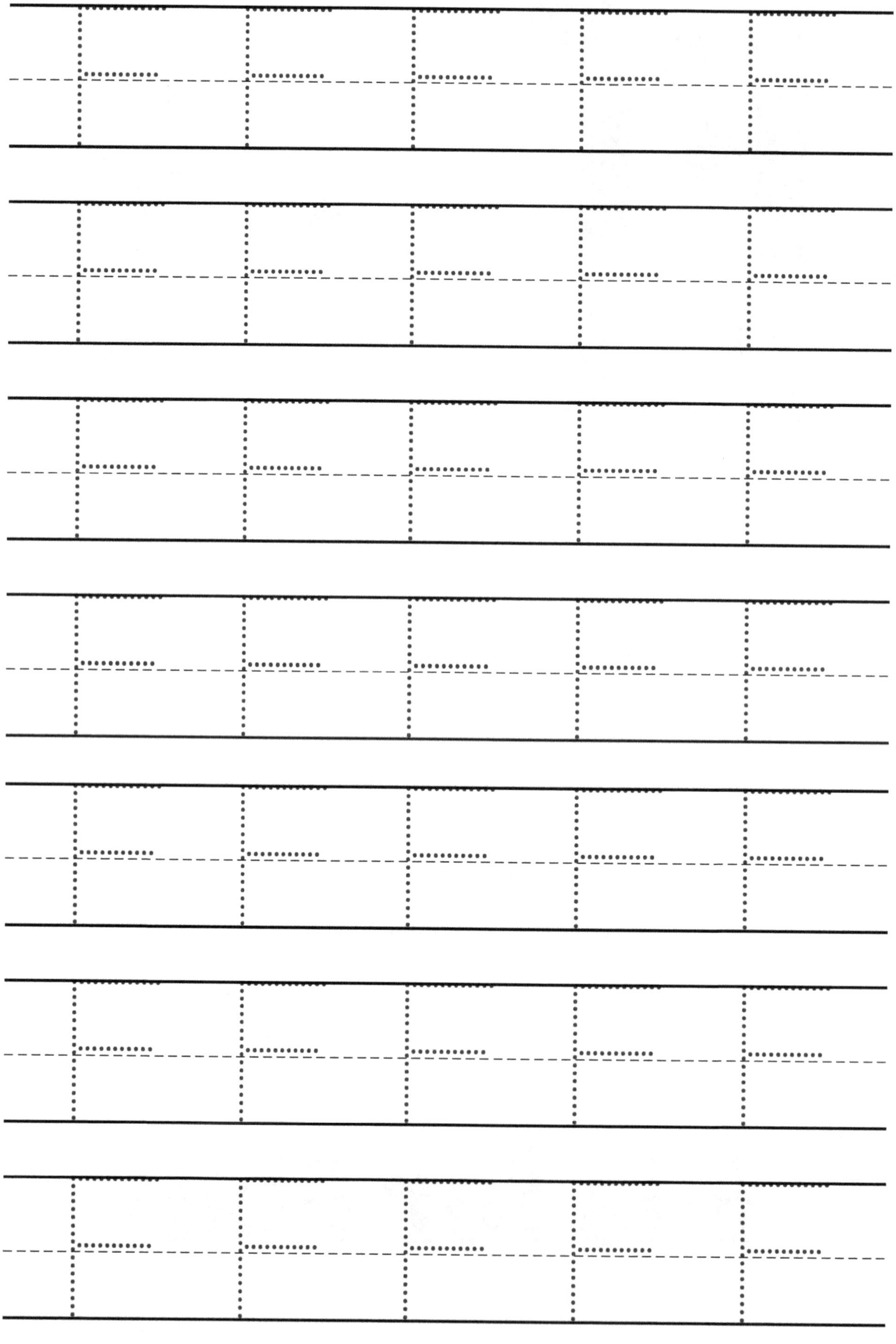

f f f f f f f f

f f f f f f f f

f f f f f f f f

f f f f f f f f

f f f f f f f f

f f f f f f f f

f f f f f f f f

Gg

giraffe

Gg

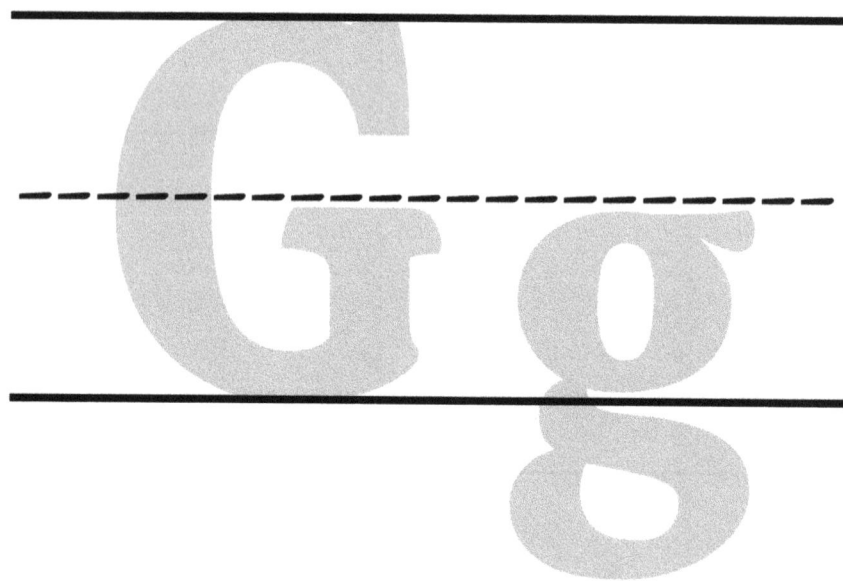

G is for Giraffe

G G G G G

G G G G G

G G G G G

G G G G G

G G G G G

G G G G G

G G G G G

g g g g g g g

g g g g g g g

g g g g g g g

g g g g g g g

g g g g g g g

g g g g g g g

g g g g g g g

Hh

house

Hh

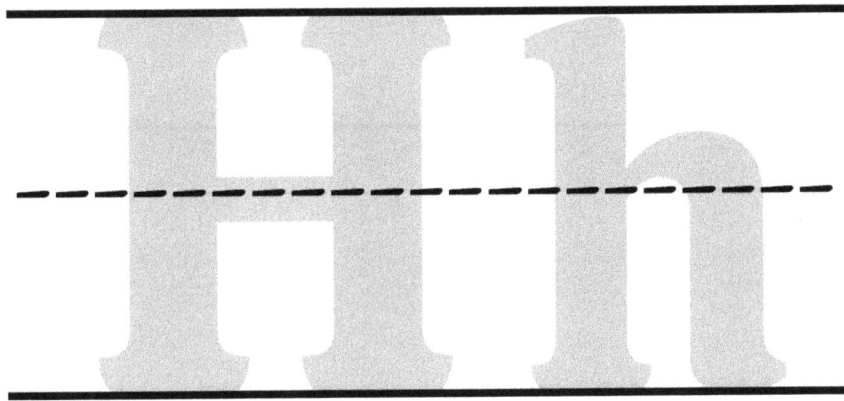

H is for House

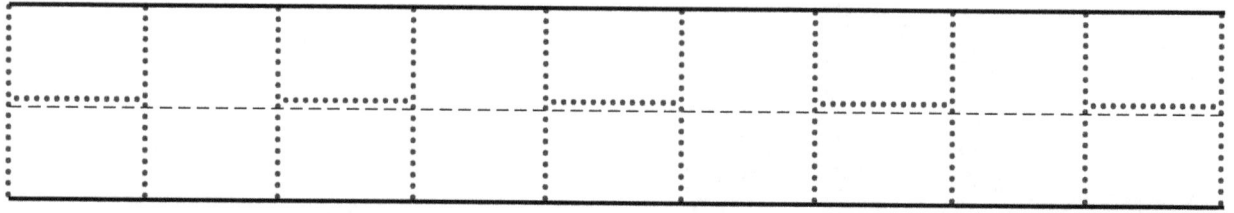

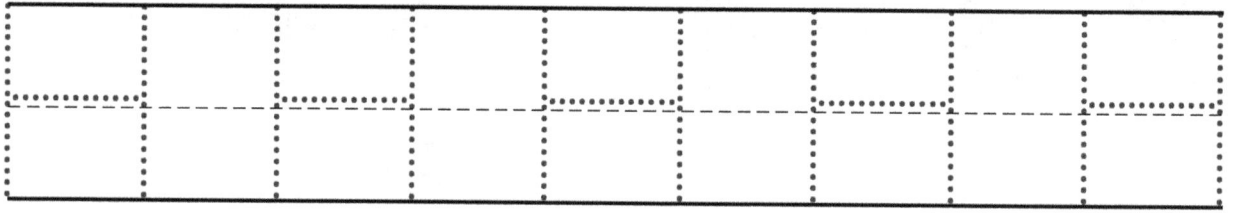

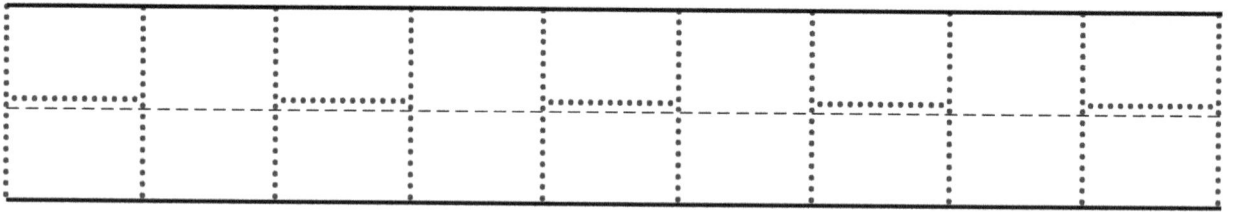

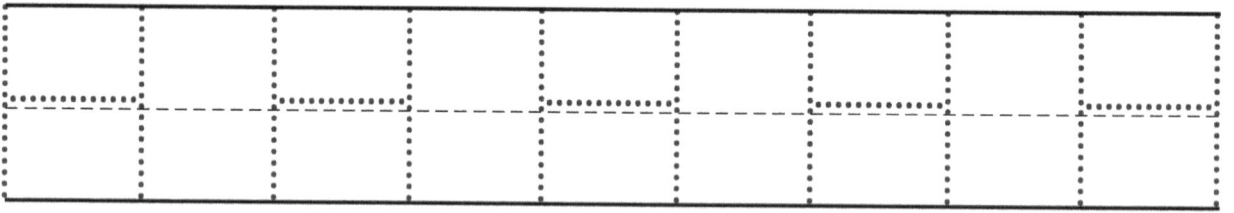

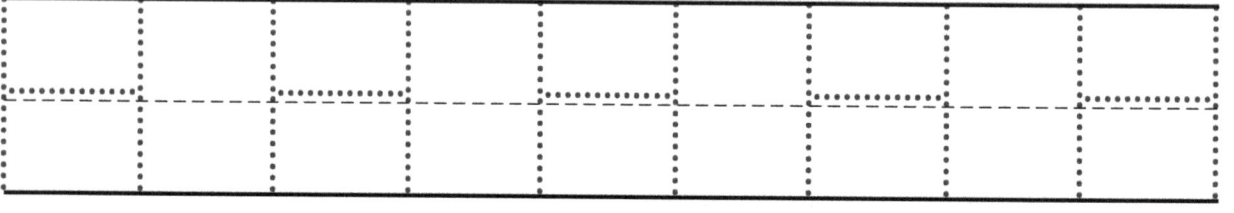

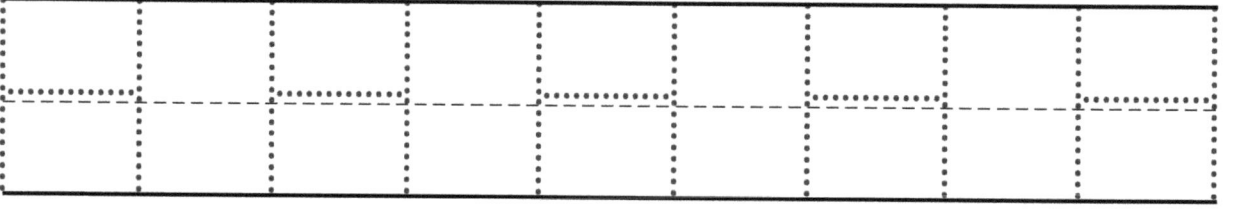

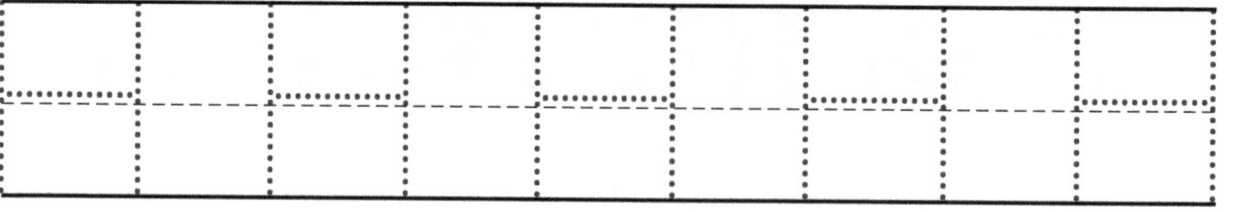

h h h h h h h

h h h h h h h

h h h h h h h

h h h h h h h

h h h h h h h

h h h h h h h

h h h h h h h

Ii

Ice Cream

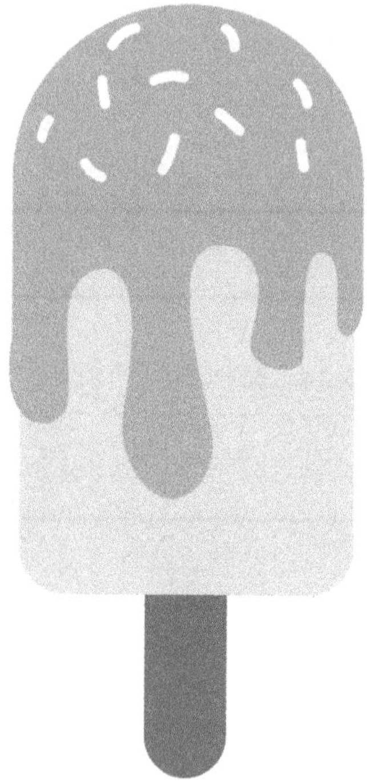

I i

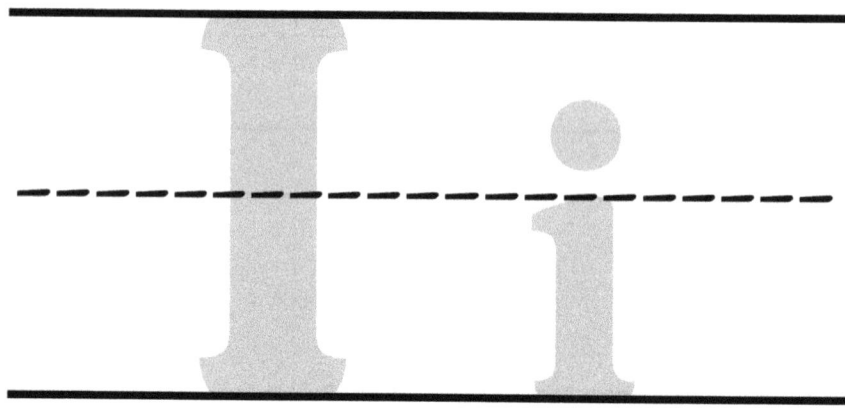

I is for Ice Cream

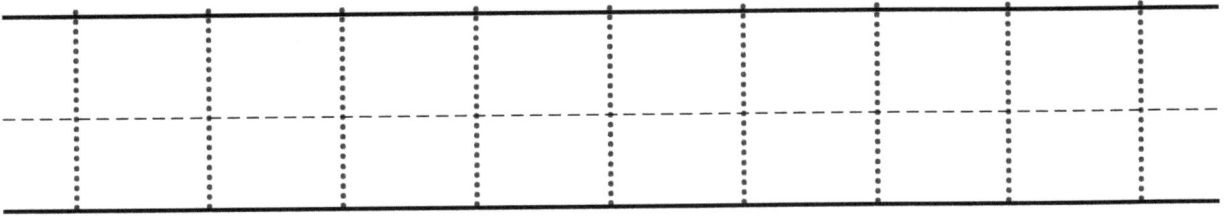

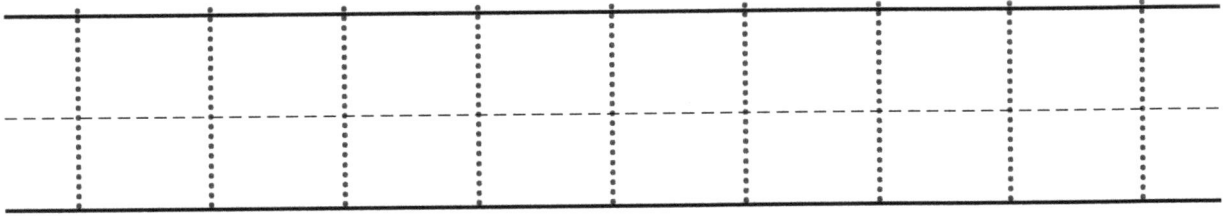

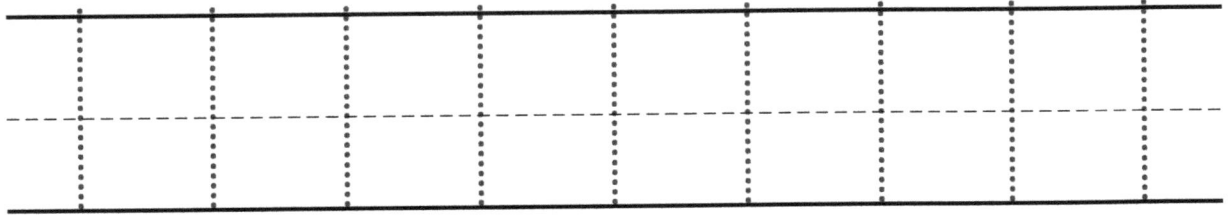

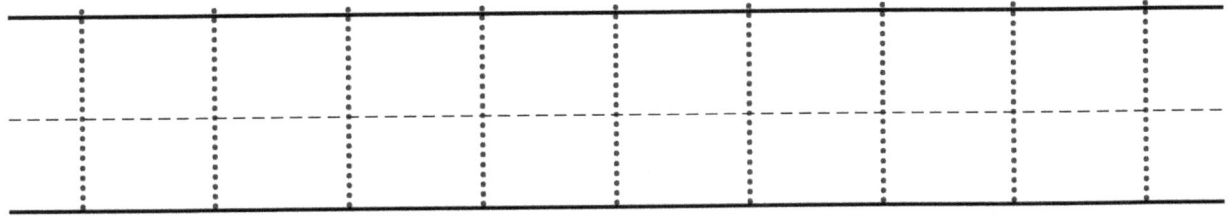

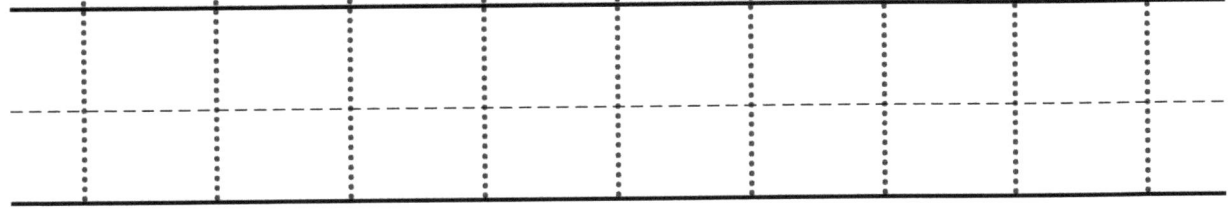

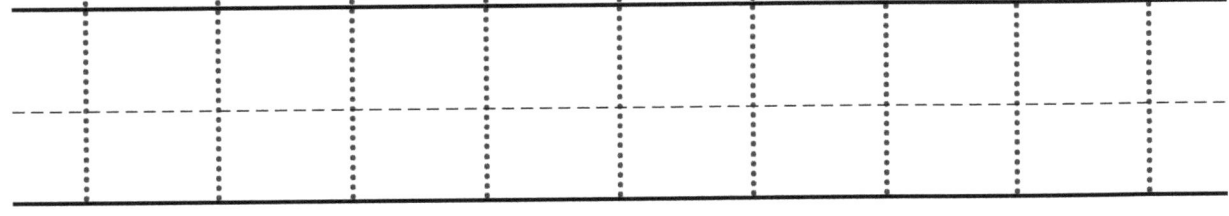

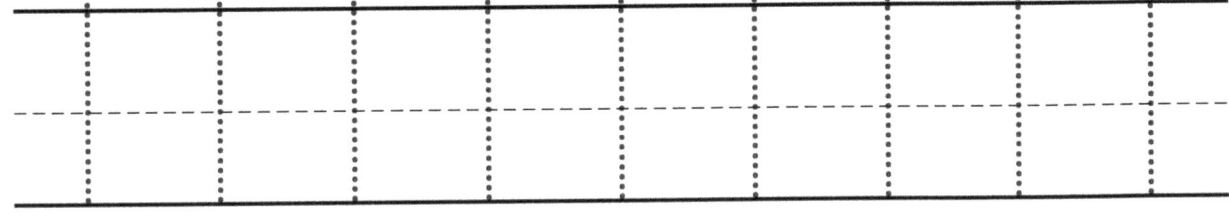

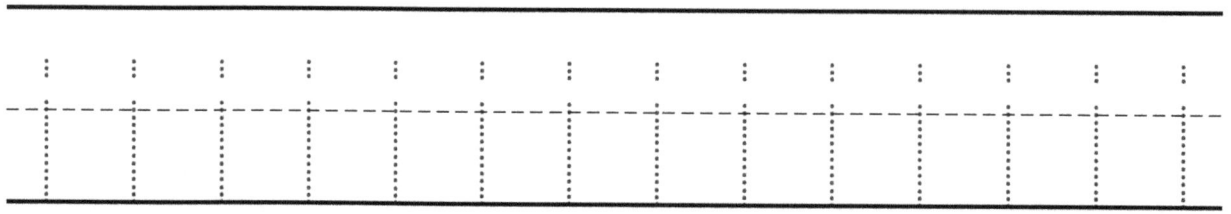

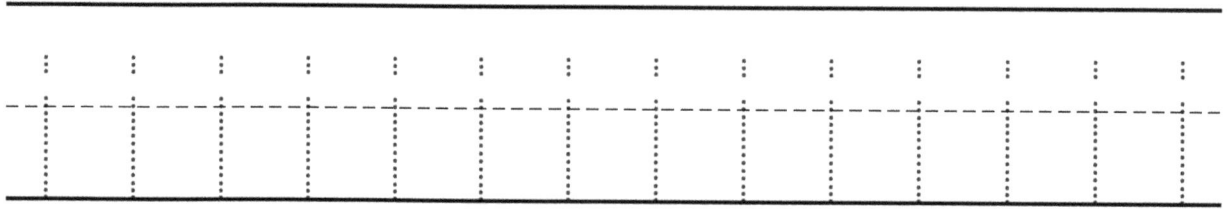

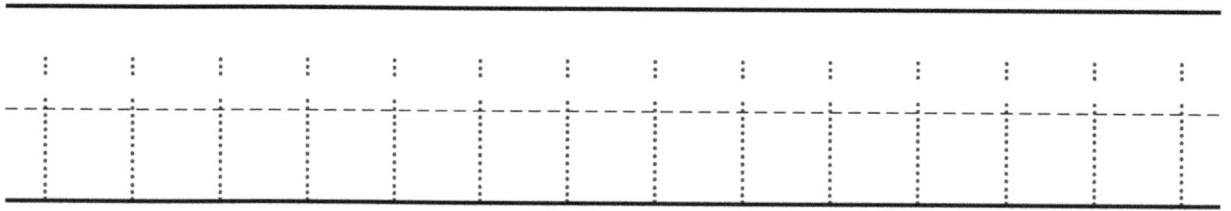

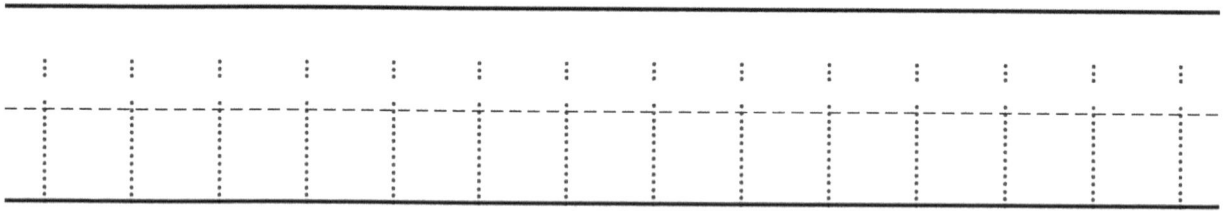

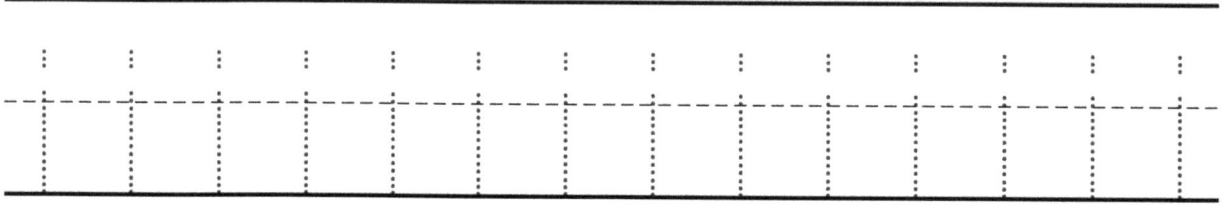

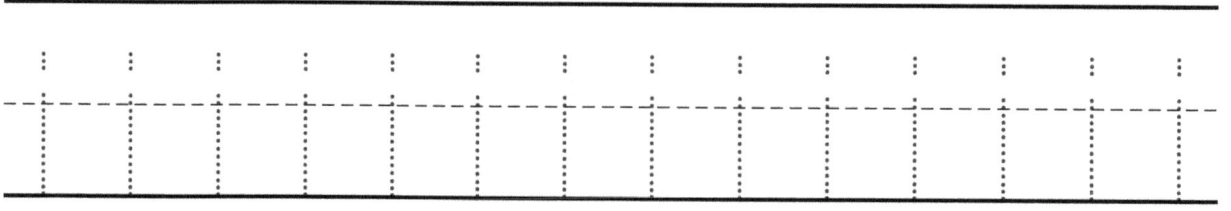

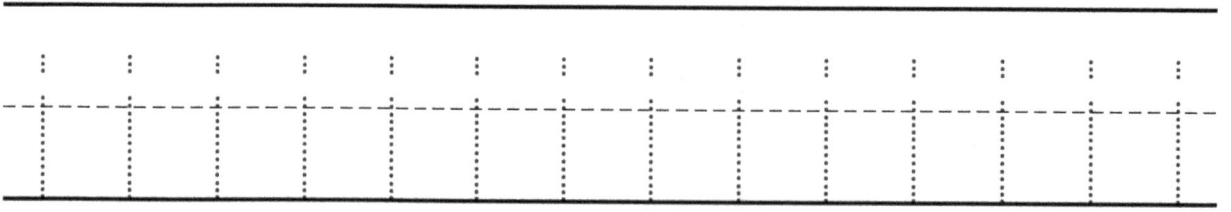

Jj

Juice

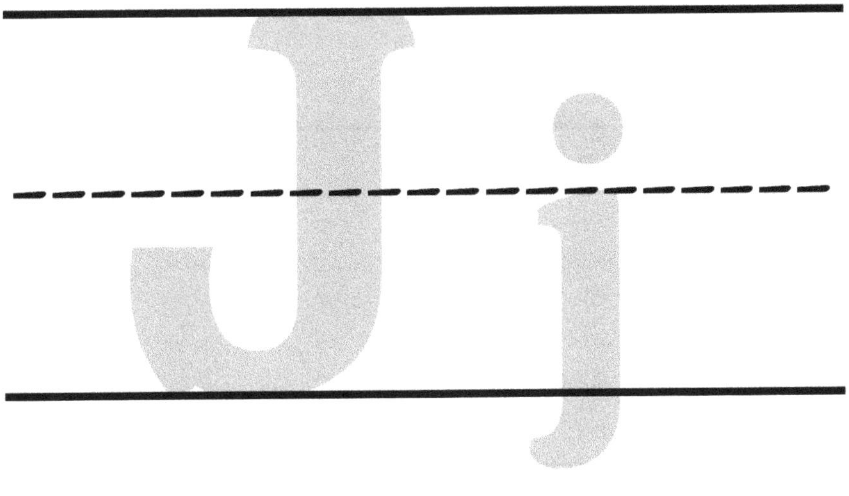

J is for Juice

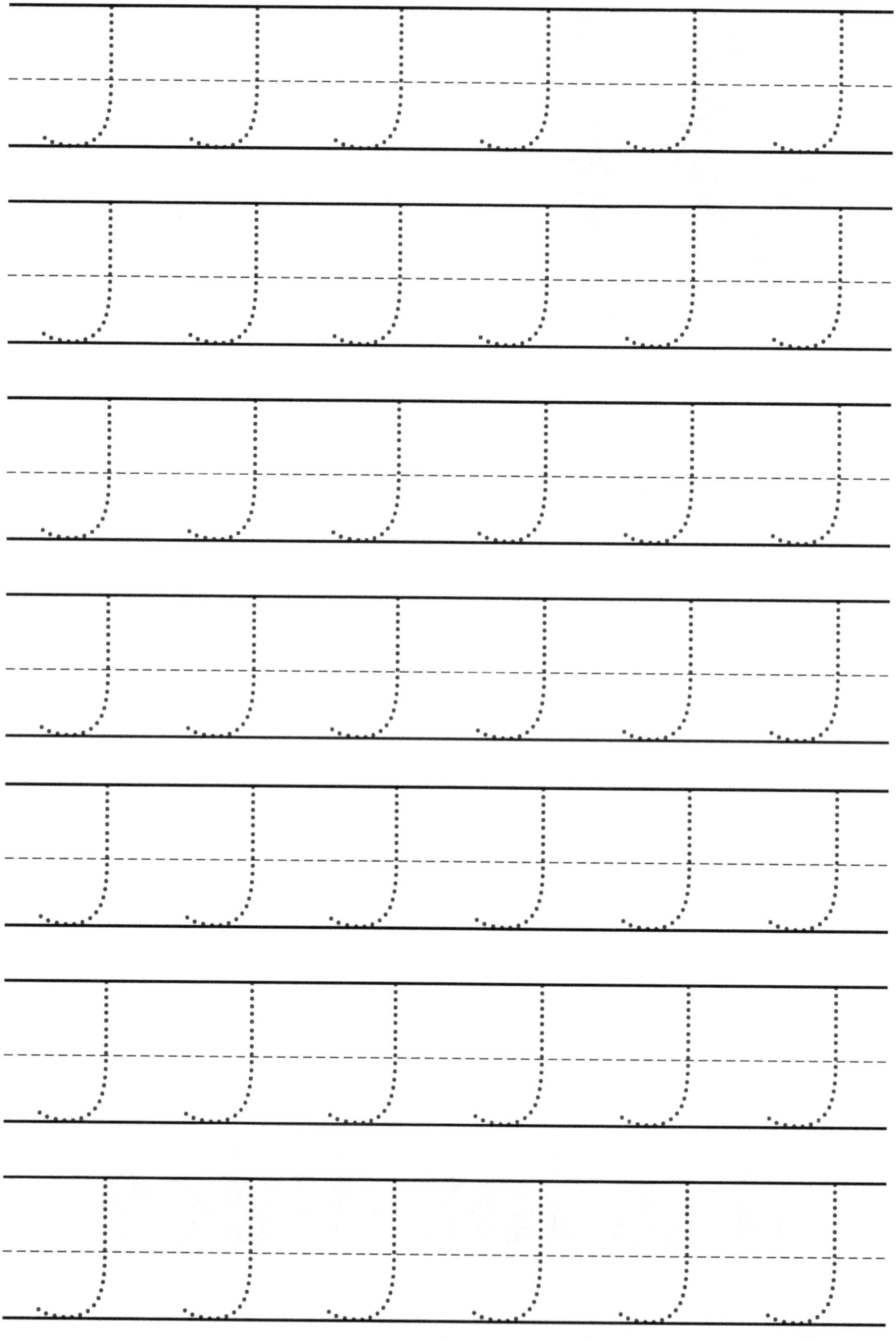

j j j j j j j j j j j j j

j j j j j j j j j j j j j

j j j j j j j j j j j j j

j j j j j j j j j j j j j

j j j j j j j j j j j j j

j j j j j j j j j j j j j

j j j j j j j j j j j j j

Kk

Kite

Kk

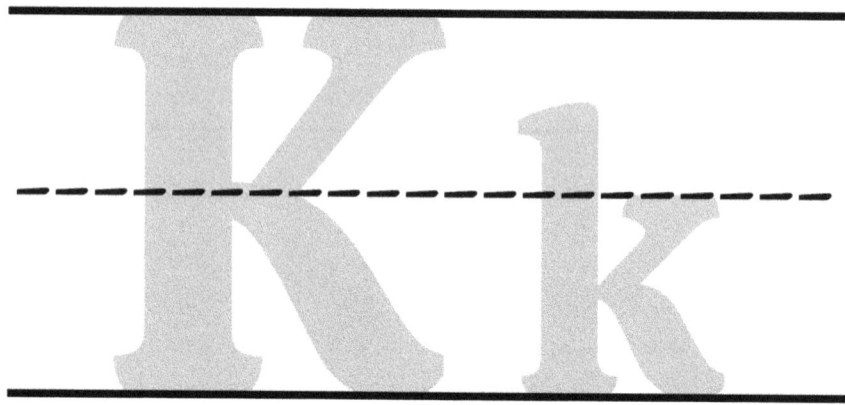

K is for Kite

K K K K K

K K K K K

K K K K K

K K K K K

K K K K K

K K K K K

K K K K K

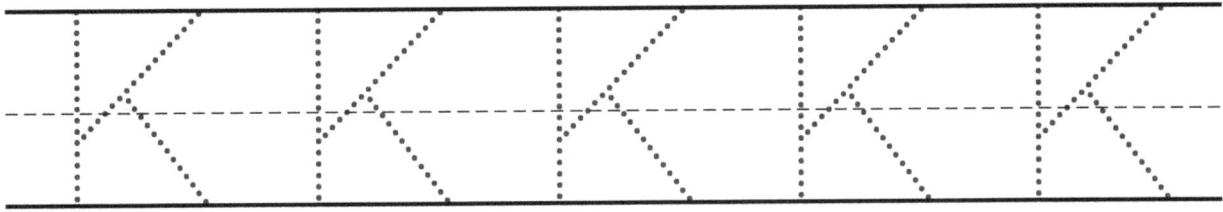

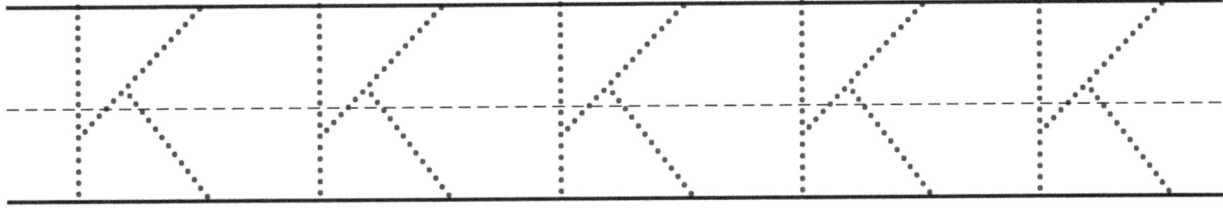

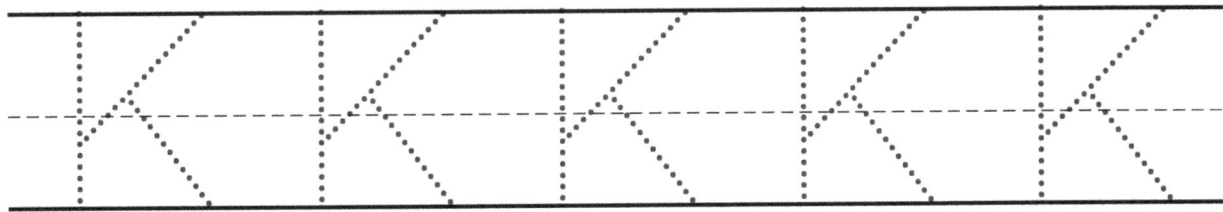

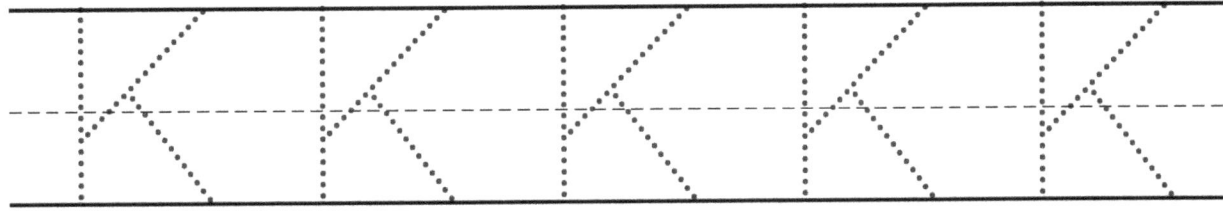

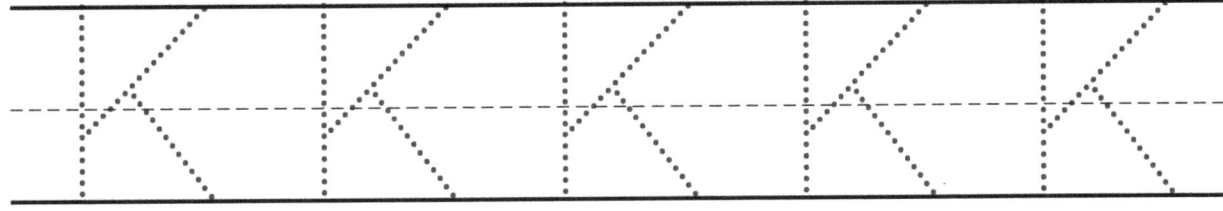

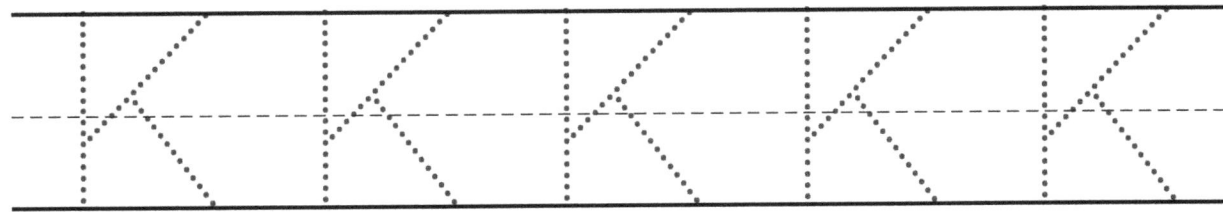

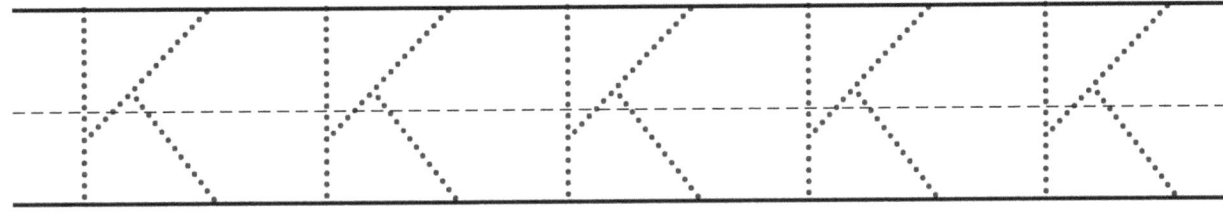

K K K K K K K

K K K K K K K

K K K K K K K

K K K K K K K

K K K K K K K

K K K K K K K

K K K K K K K

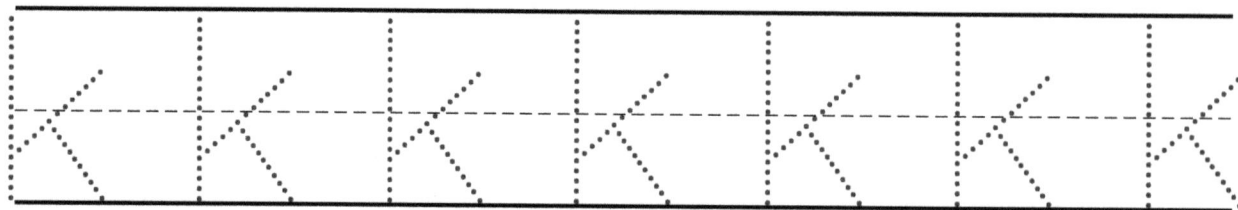

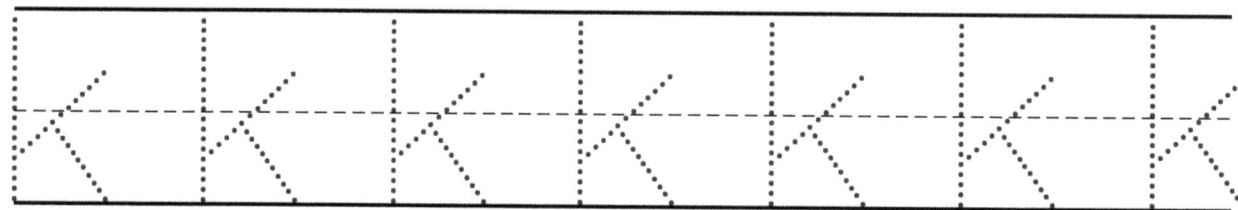

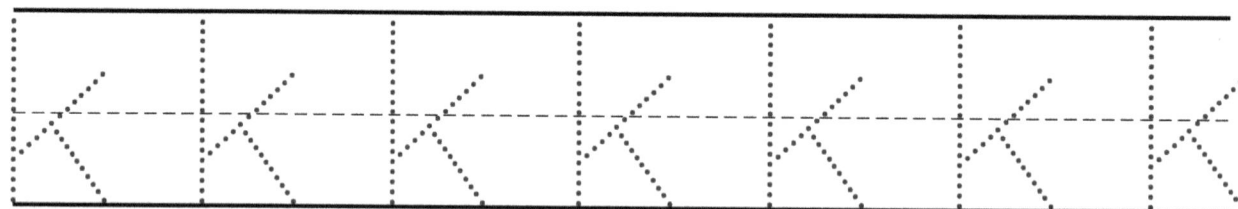

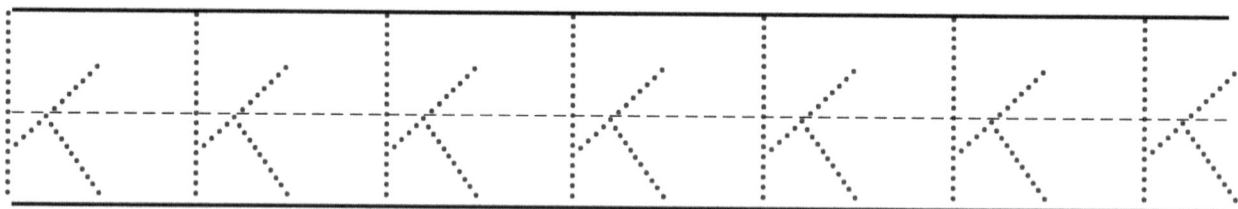

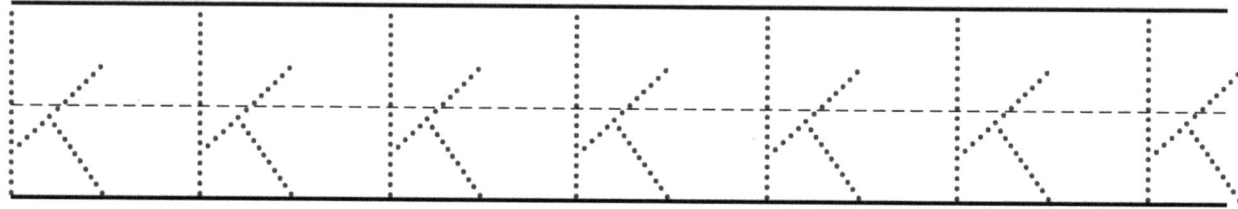

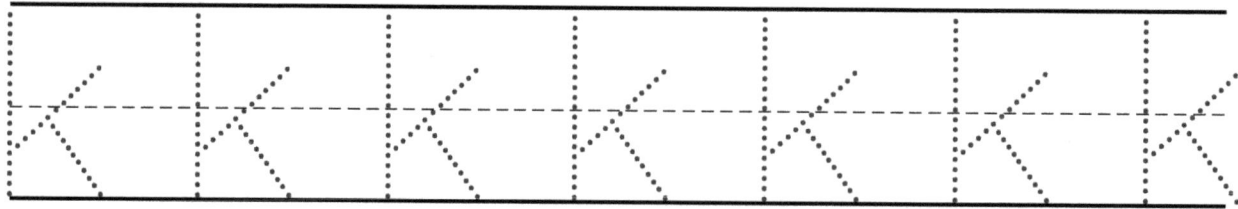

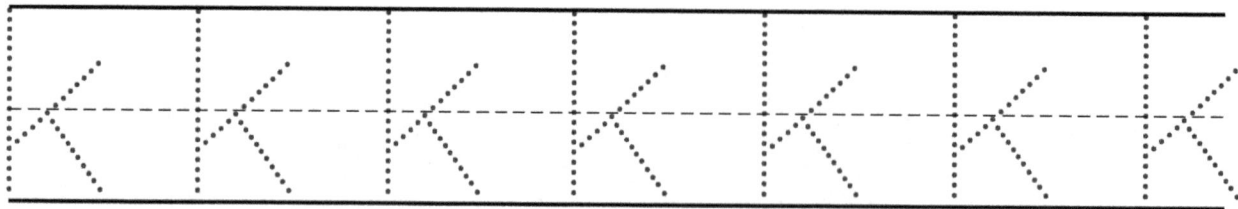

Ll

Ladybug

Ll

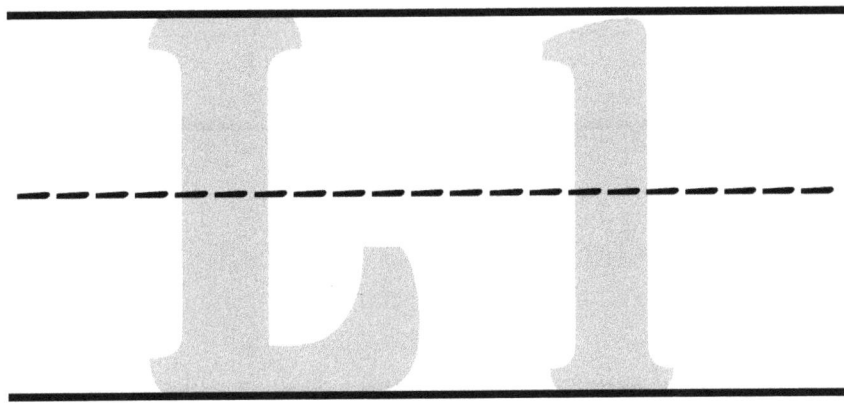

L is for Ladybug

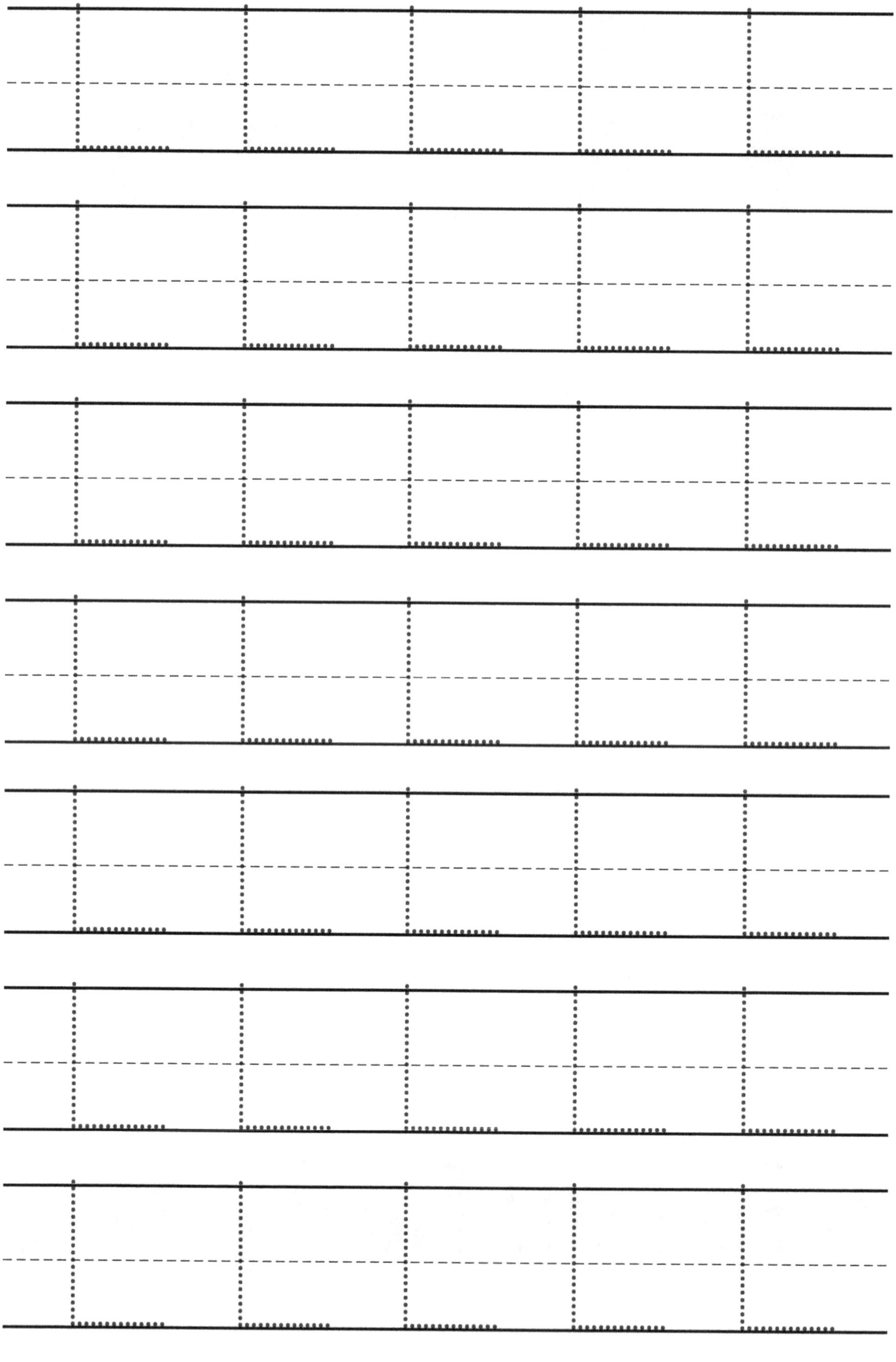

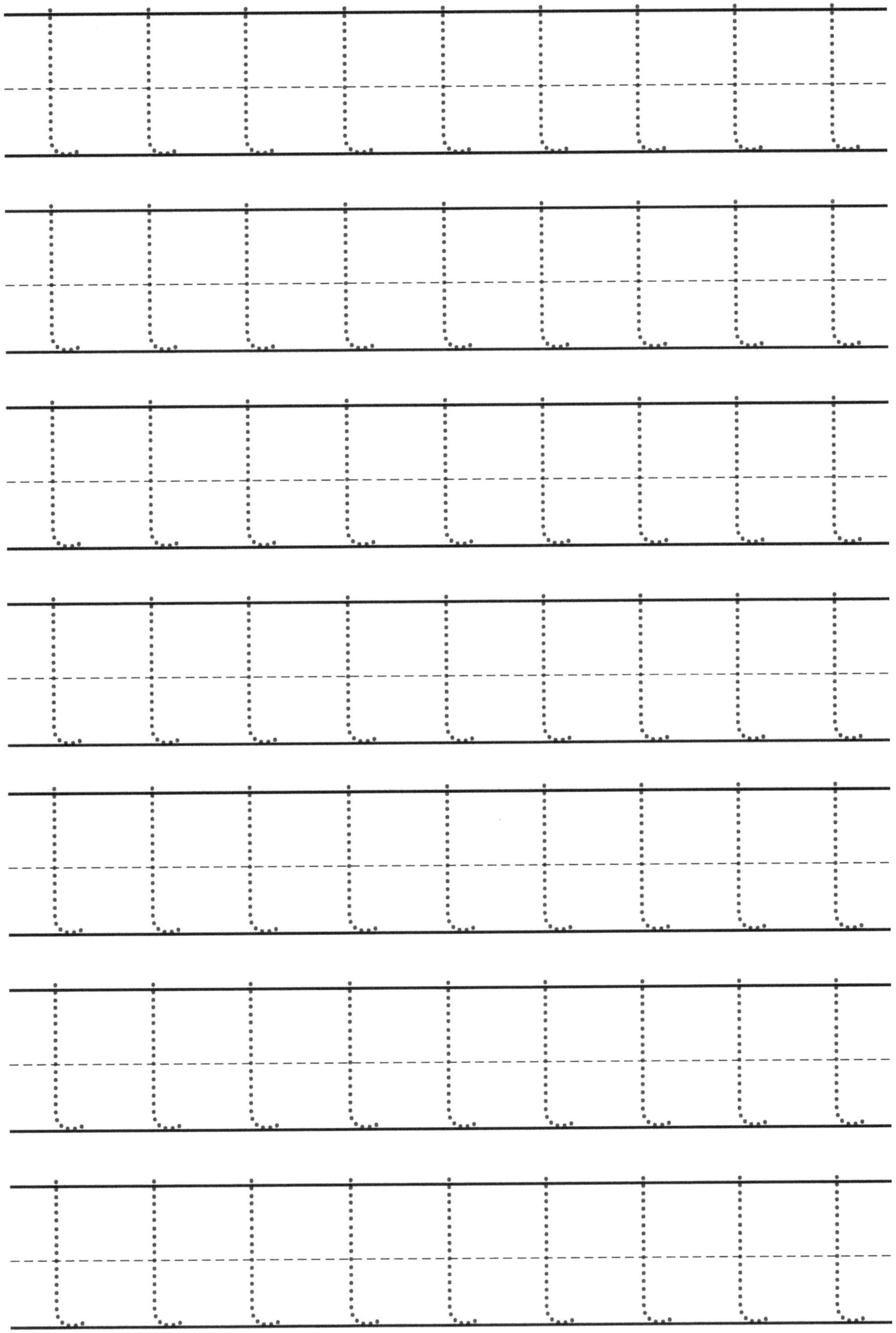

Mm

Monkey

Mm

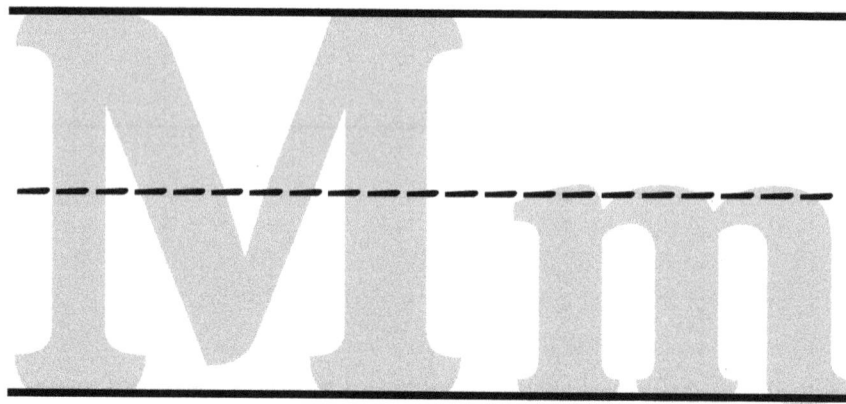

M is for Monkey

M M M M

M M M M

M M M M

M M M M

M M M M

M M M M

M M M M

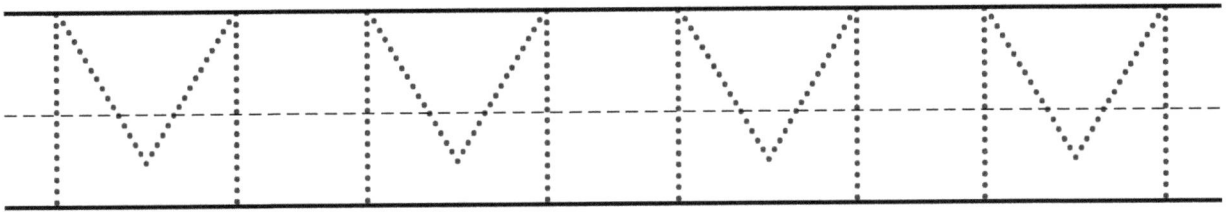

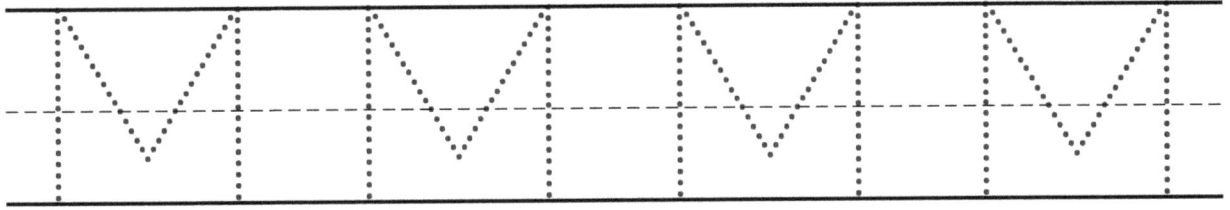

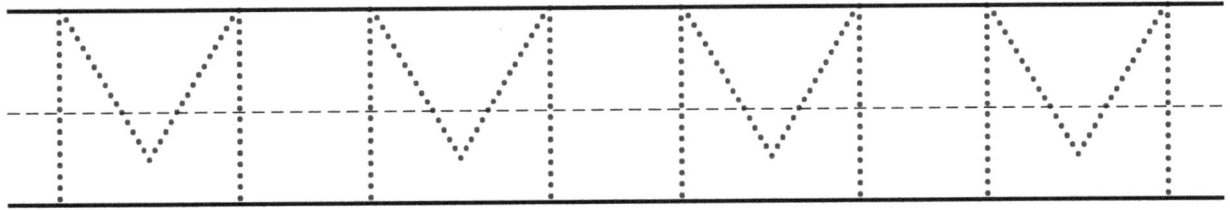

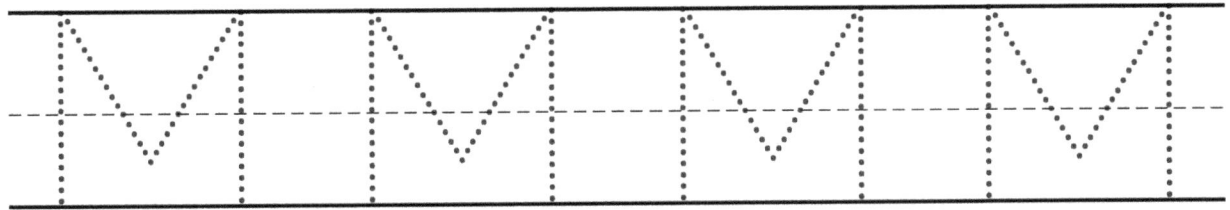

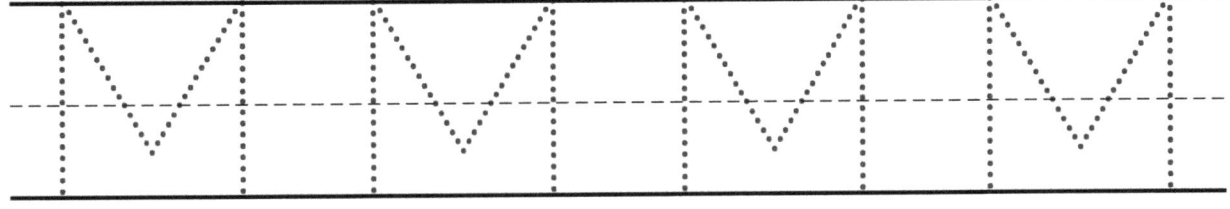

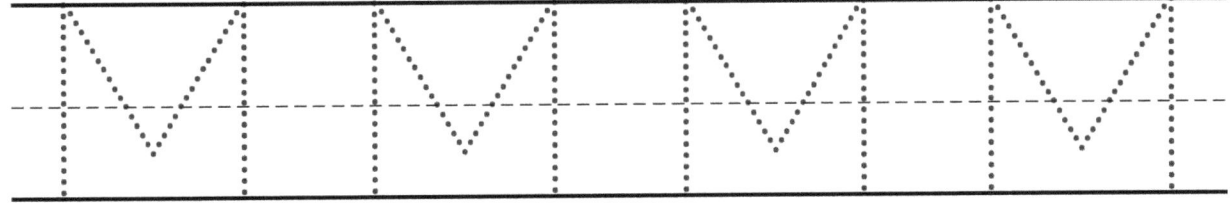

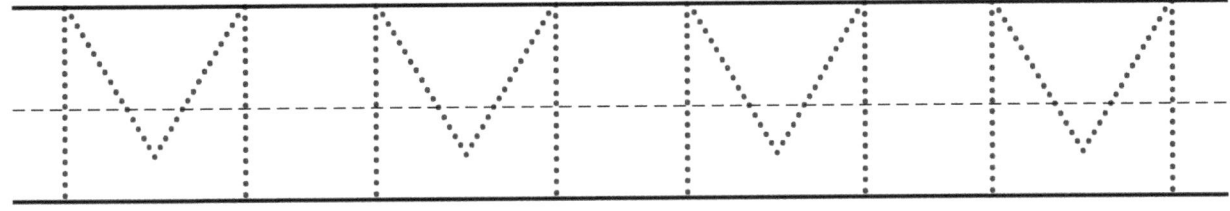

m m m m m m

m m m m m m

m m m m m m

m m m m m m

m m m m m m

m m m m m m

m m m m m m

m m m m m m

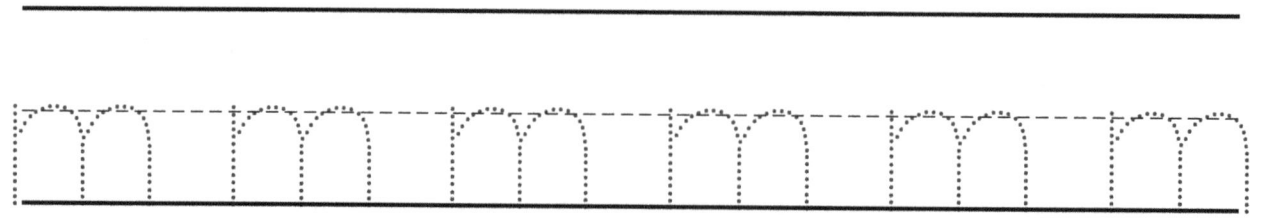

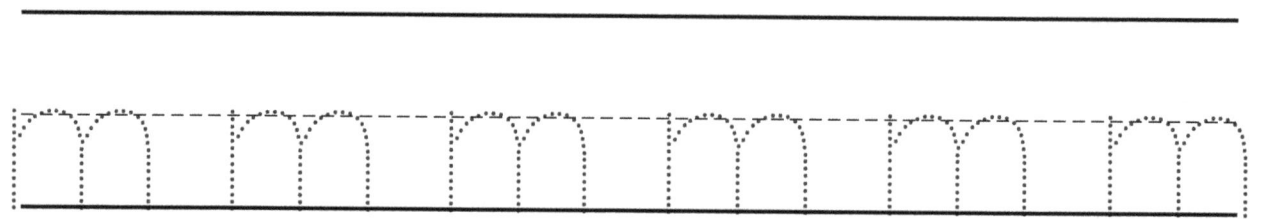

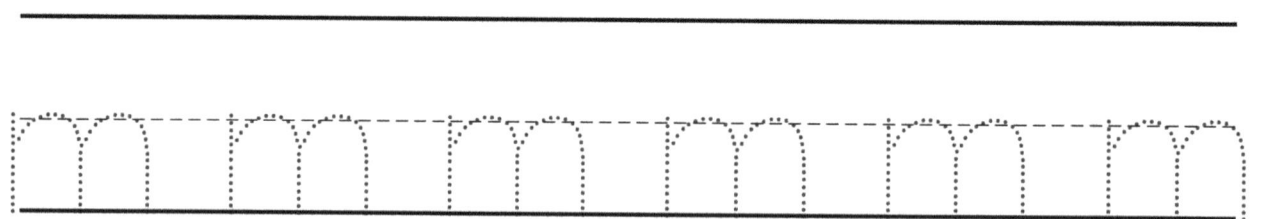

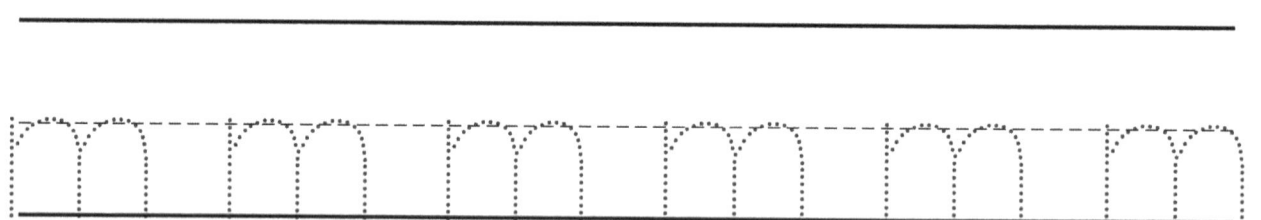

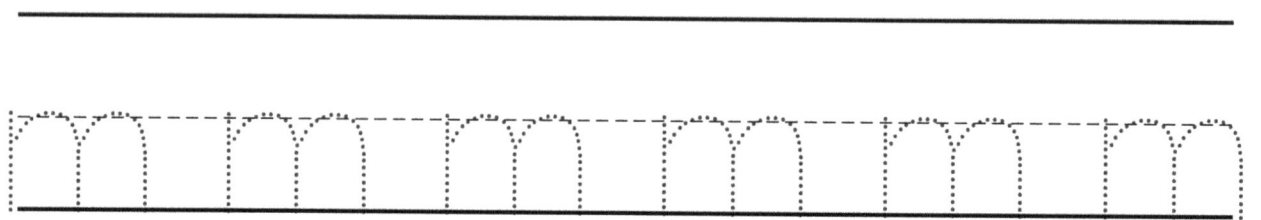

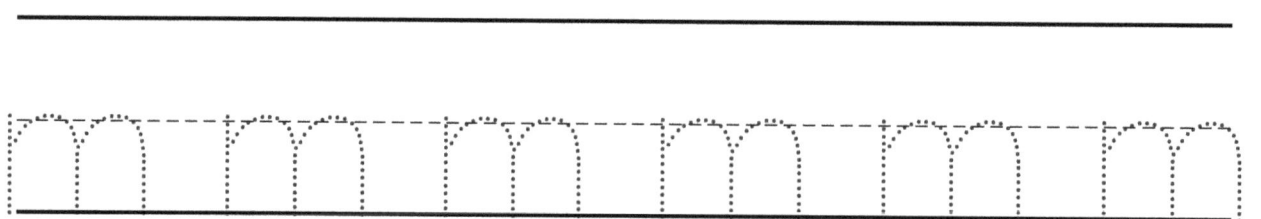

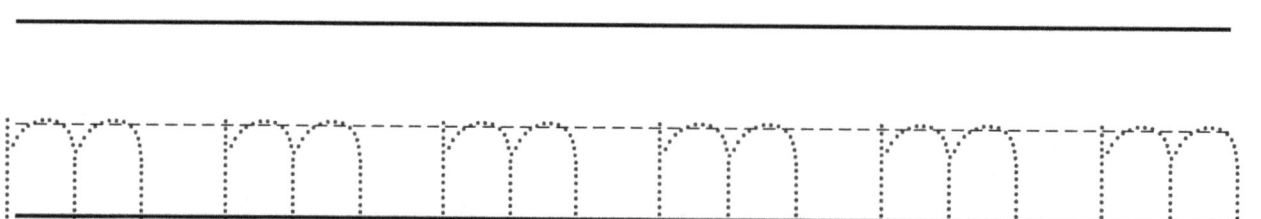

Nn

Nest

N n

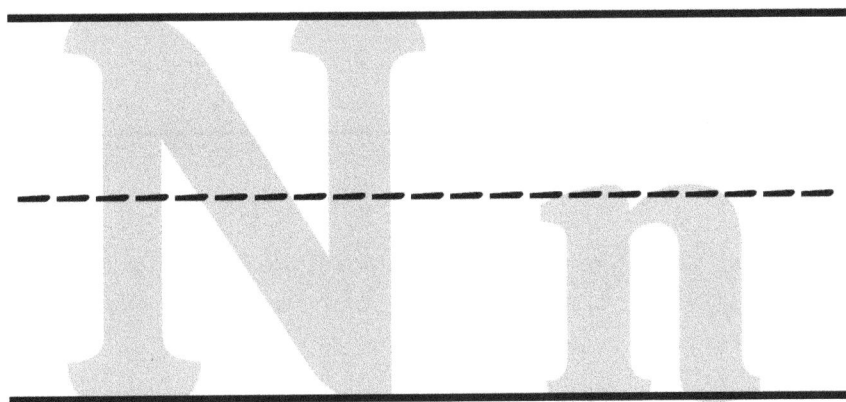

N is for Nest

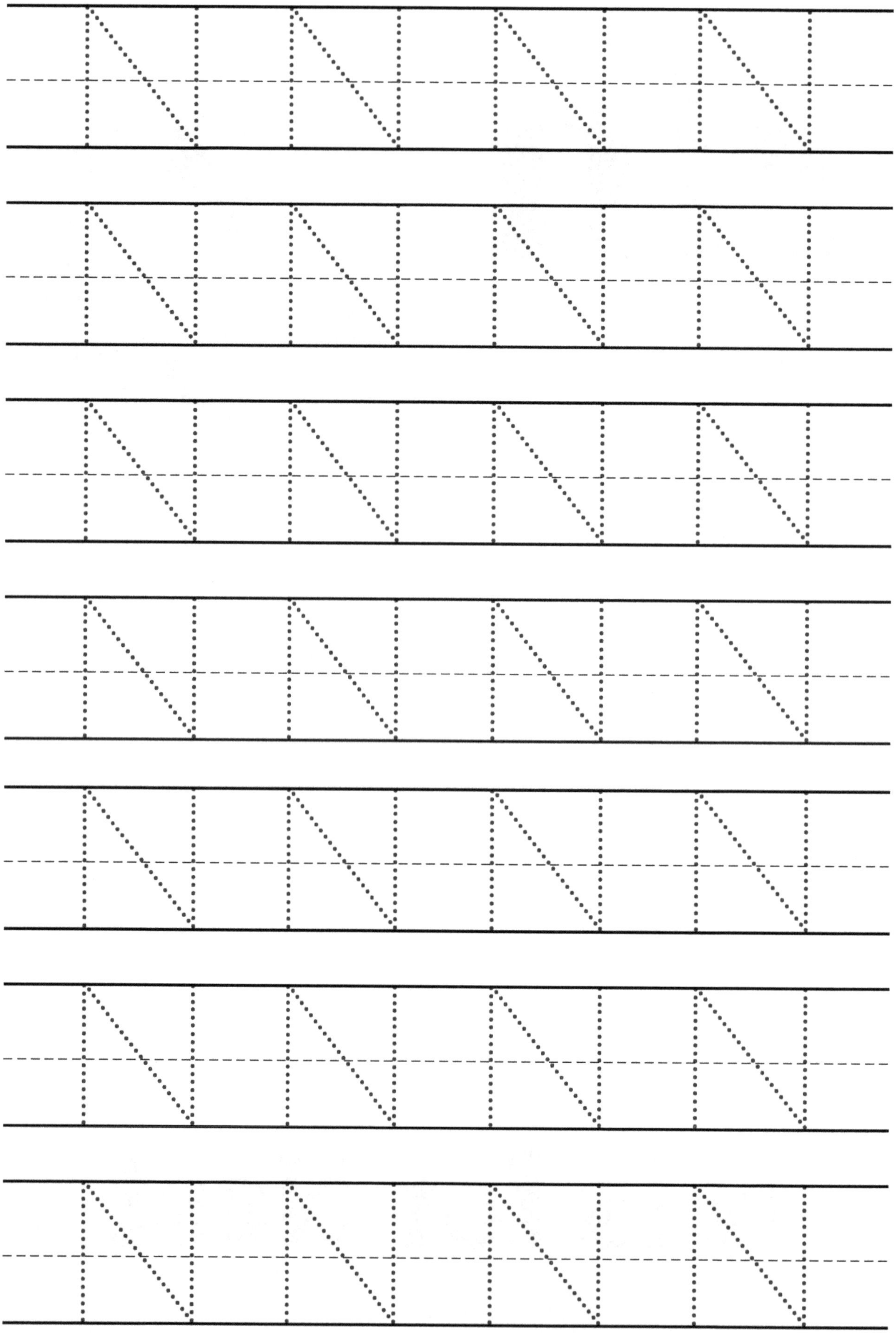

n n n n n n n n

n n n n n n n n

n n n n n n n n

n n n n n n n n

n n n n n n n n

n n n n n n n n

n n n n n n n n

Oo

Orange

O o

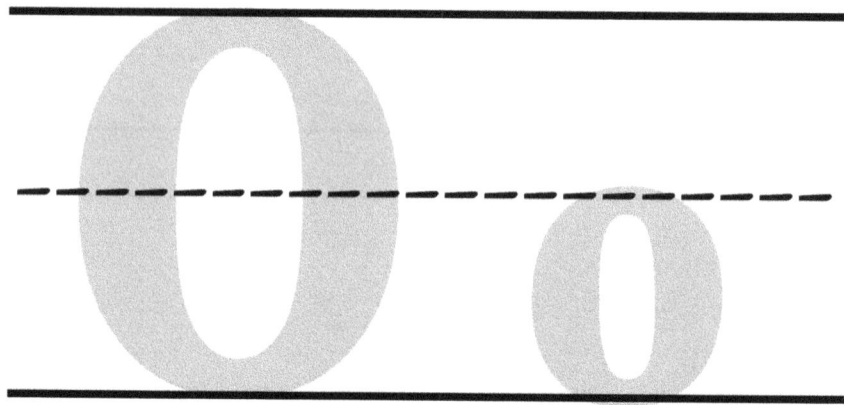

O is for Orange

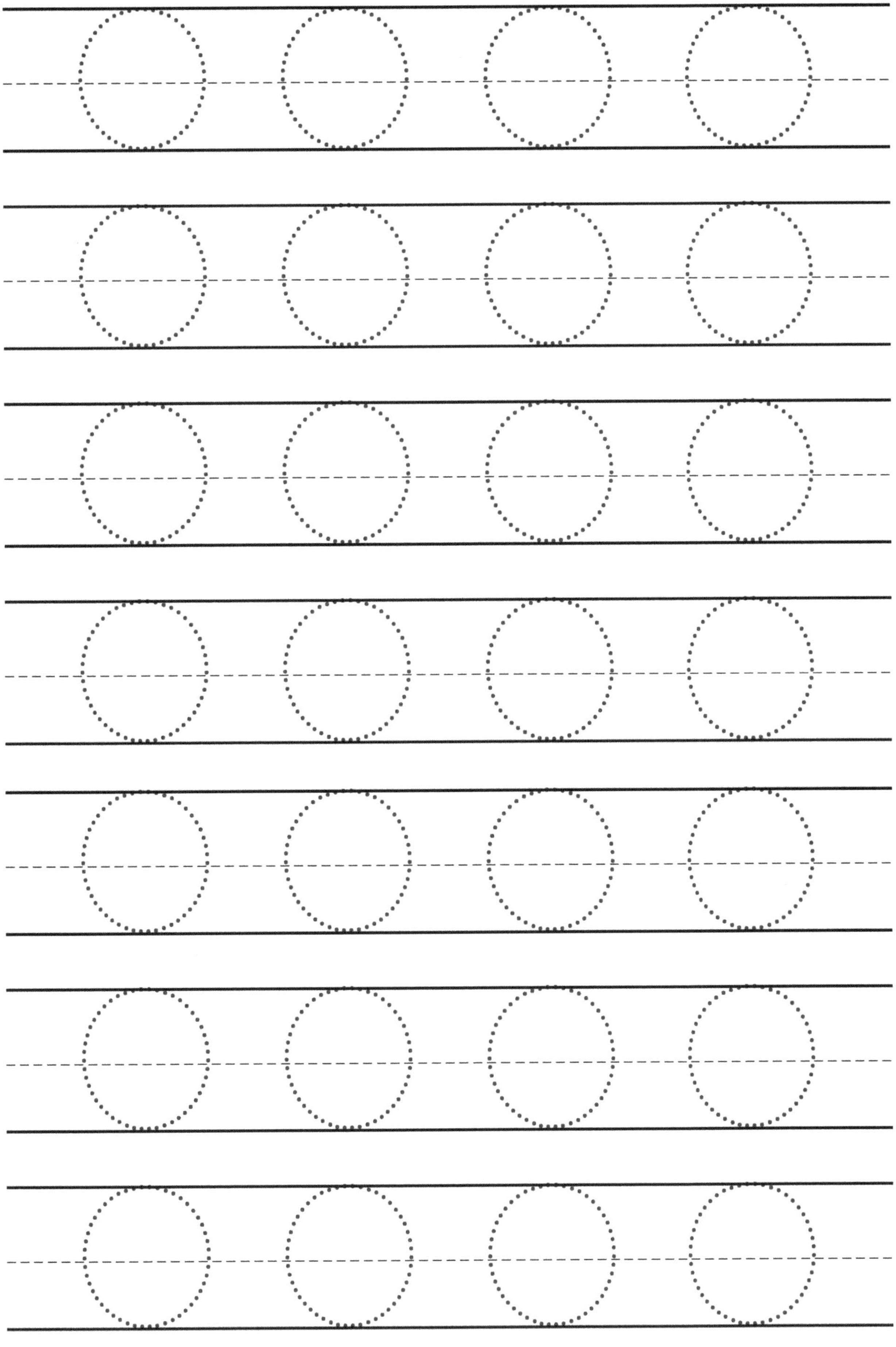

Pp

Penguin

P p

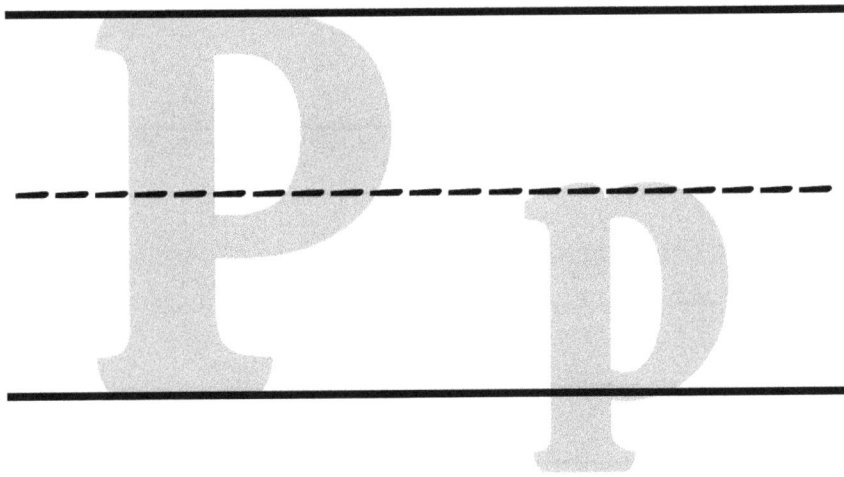

P is for Penguin

P P P P P

P P P P P

P P P P P

P P P P P

P P P P P

P P P P P

P P P P P

p p p p p p p p

p p p p p p p p

p p p p p p p p

p p p p p p p p

p p p p p p p p

p p p p p p p p

p p p p p p p p

Qq

Question

Q q

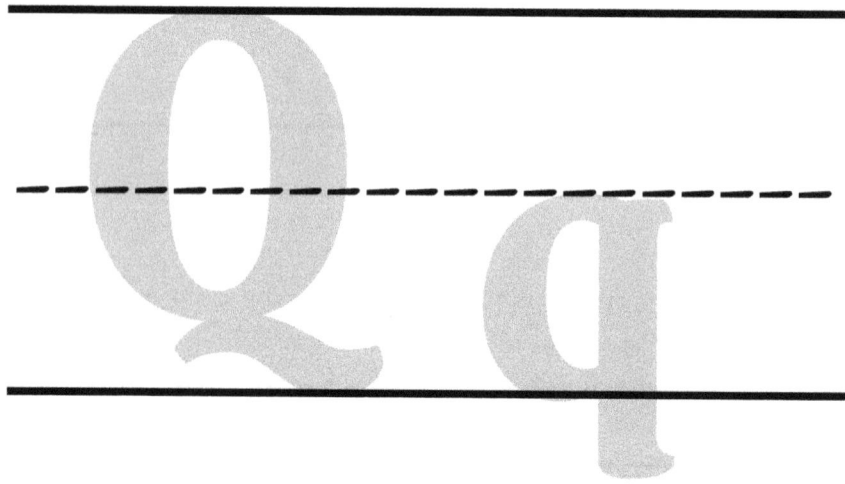

Q is for Question

Q Q Q Q

Q Q Q Q

Q Q Q Q

Q Q Q Q

Q Q Q Q

Q Q Q Q

Q Q Q Q

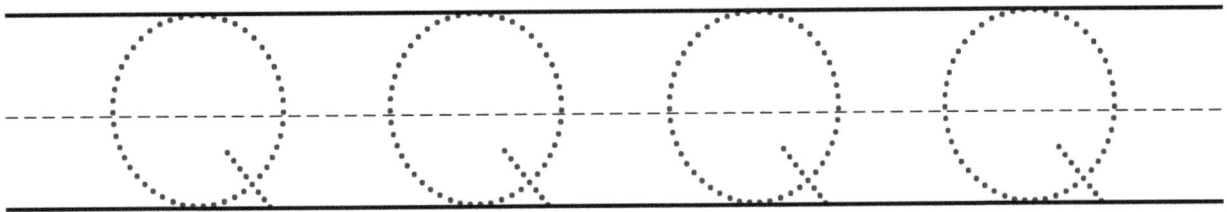

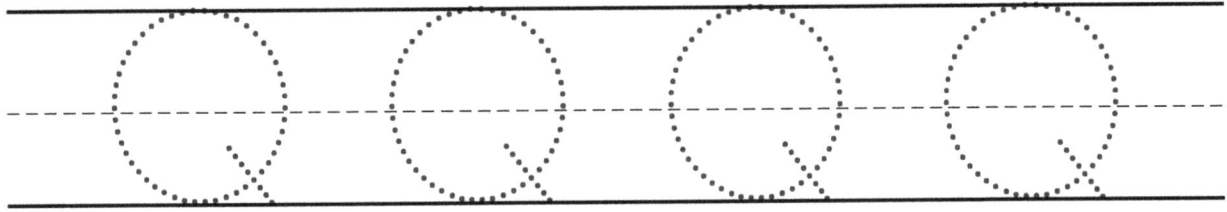

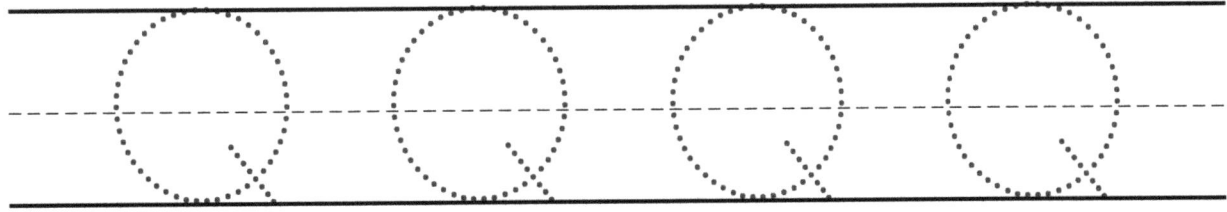

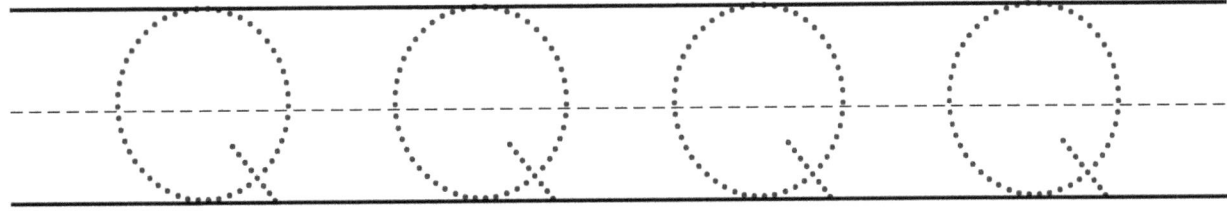

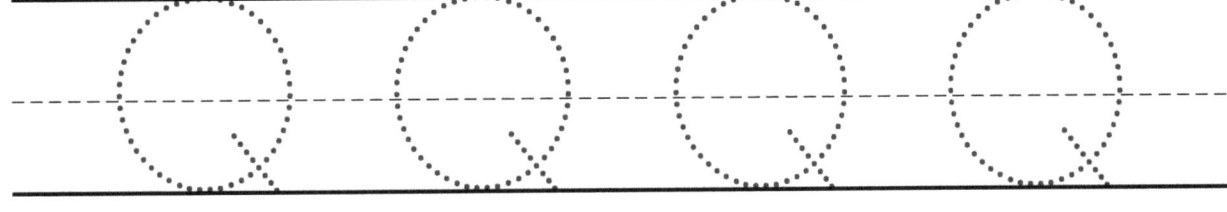

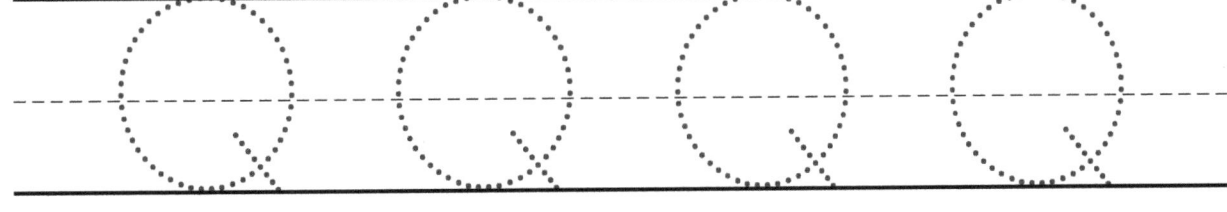

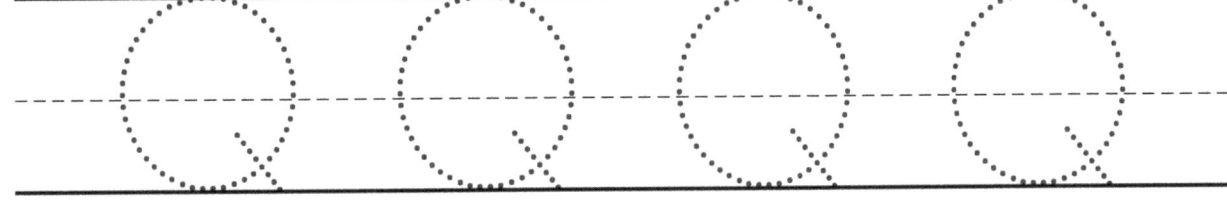

q q q q q q q

q q q q q q q

q q q q q q q

q q q q q q q

q q q q q q q

q q q q q q q

q q q q q q q

q q q q q q q

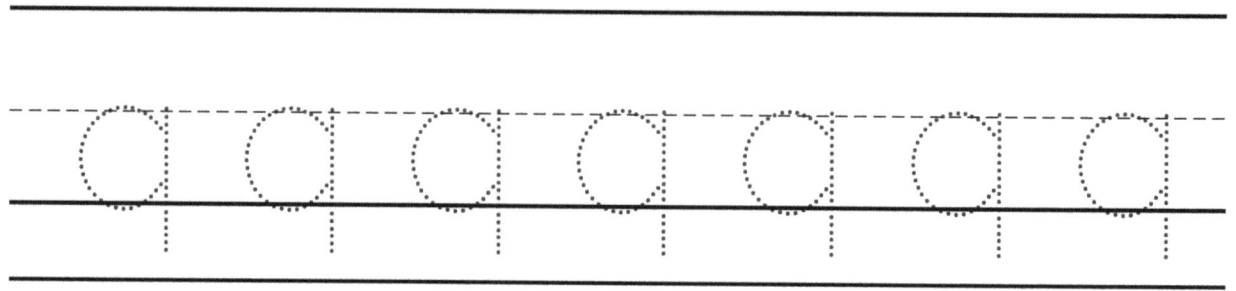

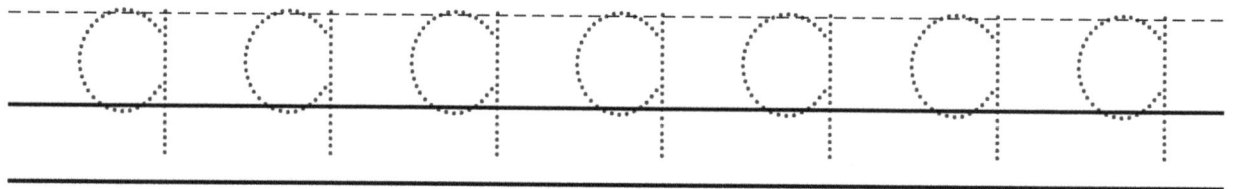

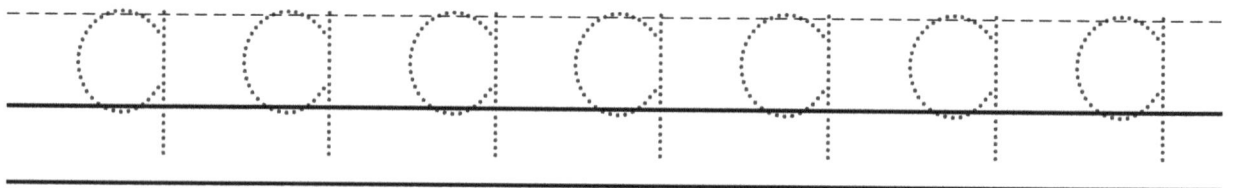

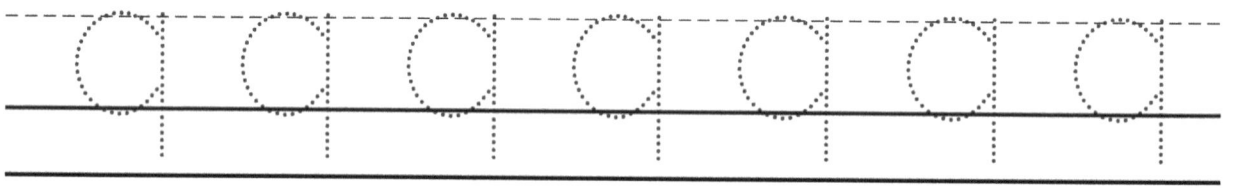

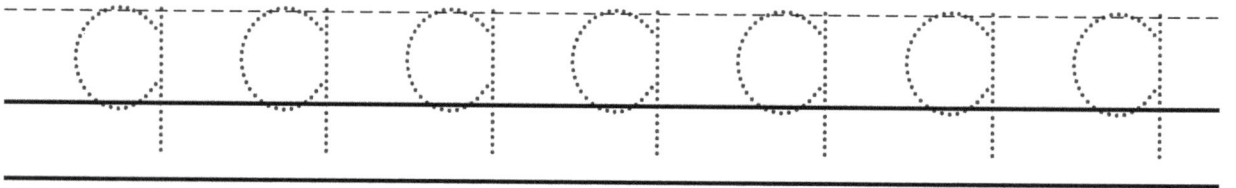

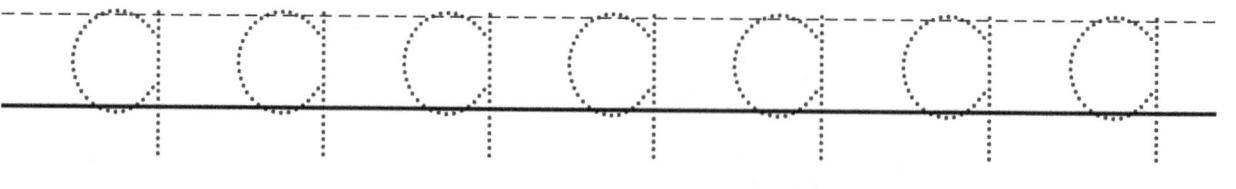

Rr

Rocket

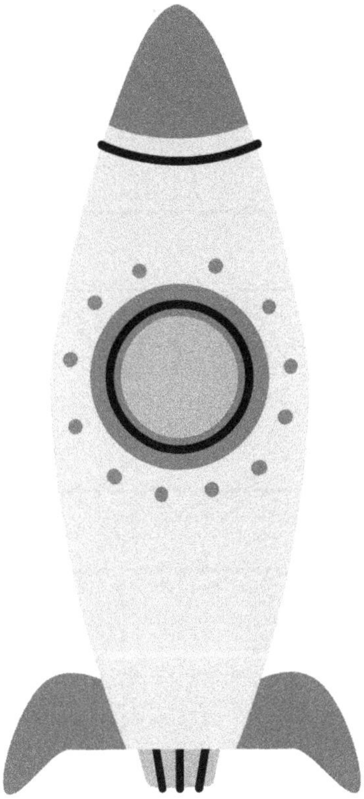

Rr

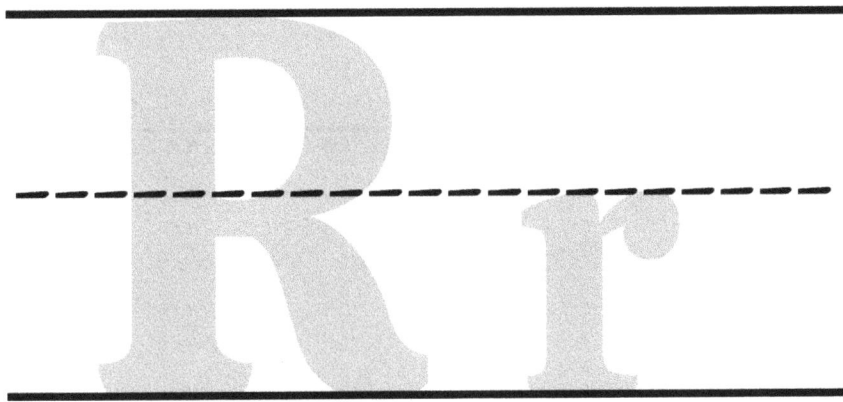

R is for Rocket

R R R R R

R R R R R

R R R R R

R R R R R

R R R R R

R R R R R

R R R R R

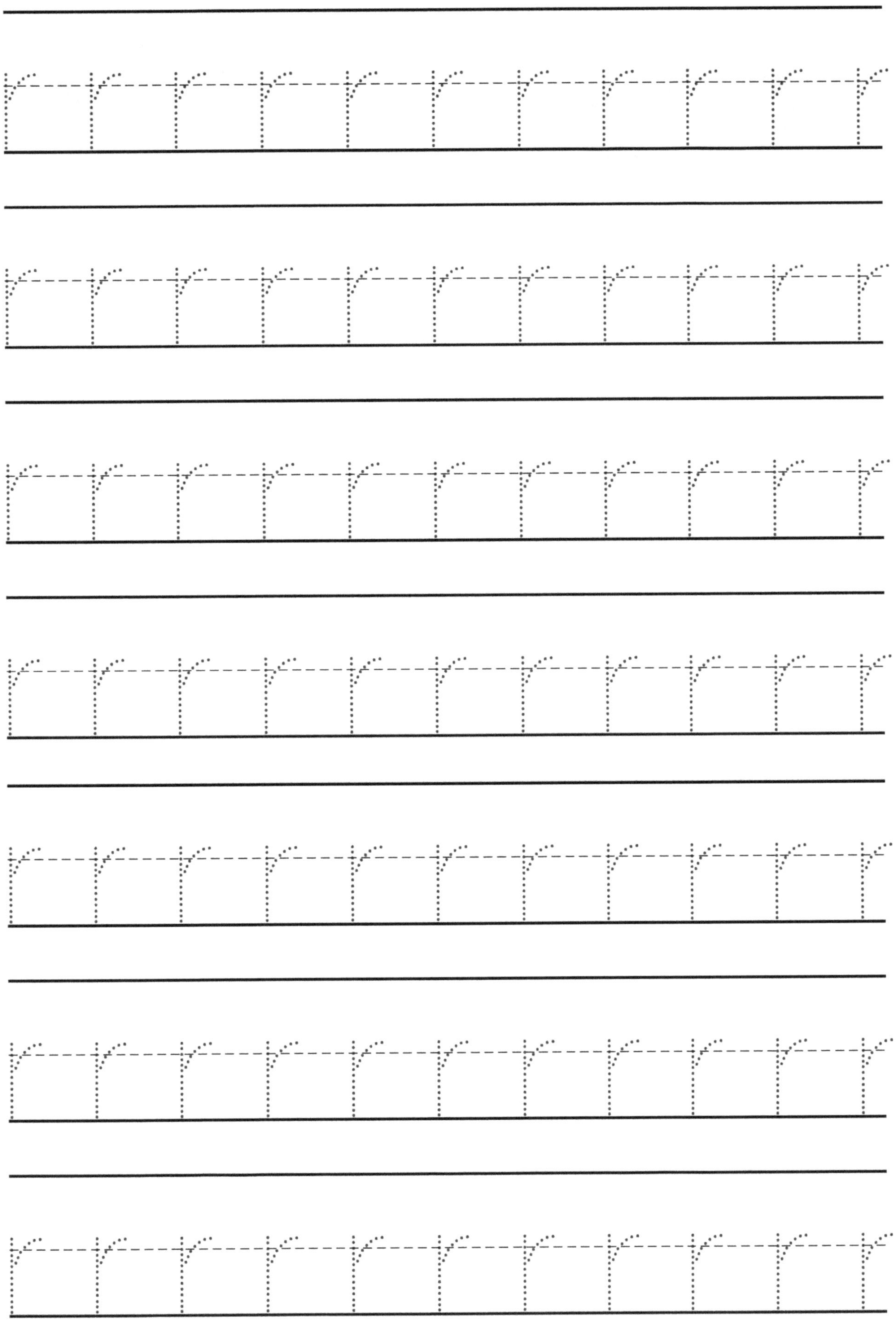

Ss

Sun

S s

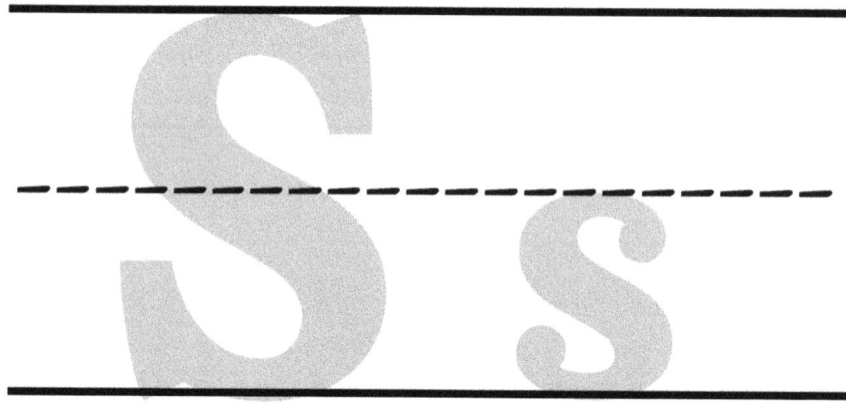

S is for Sun

S S S S S

S S S S S

S S S S S

S S S S S

S S S S S

S S S S S

S S S S S

s s s s s s s s s

s s s s s s s s s

s s s s s s s s s

s s s s s s s s s

s s s s s s s s s

s s s s s s s s s

s s s s s s s s s

Tt

Tree

T t

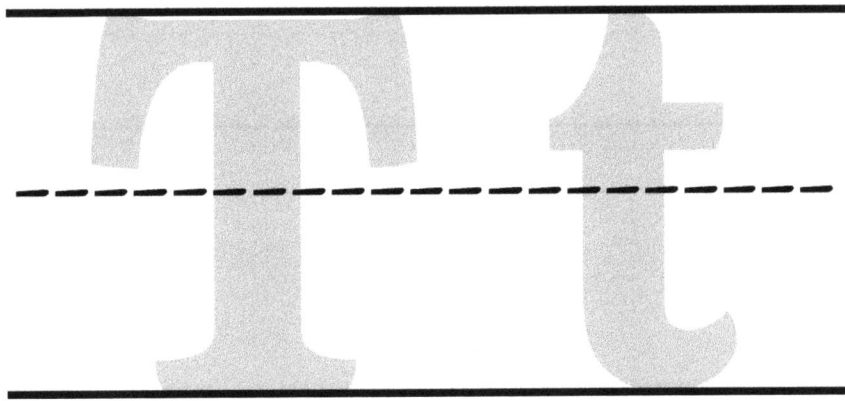

T is for Tree

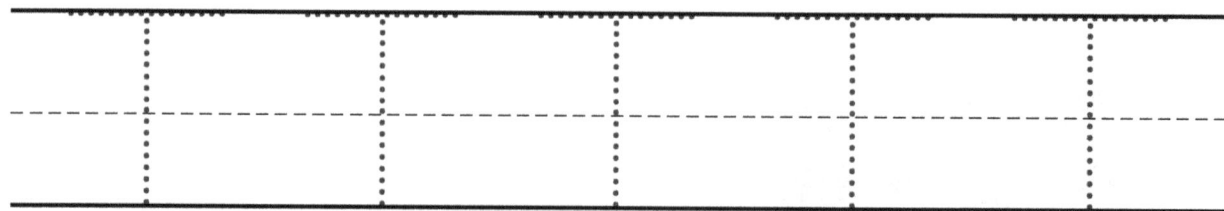

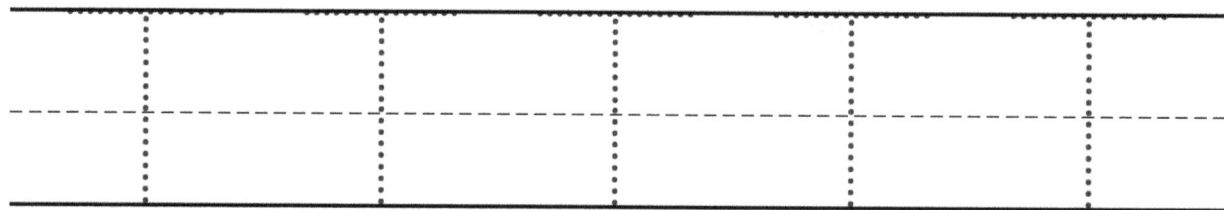

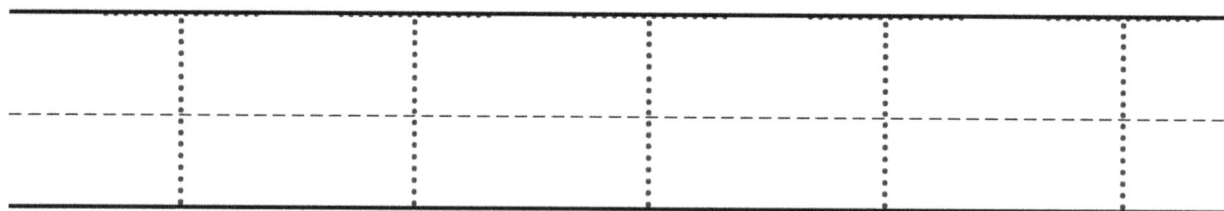

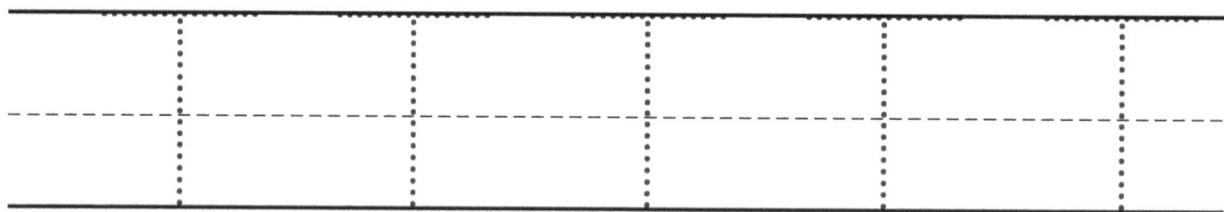

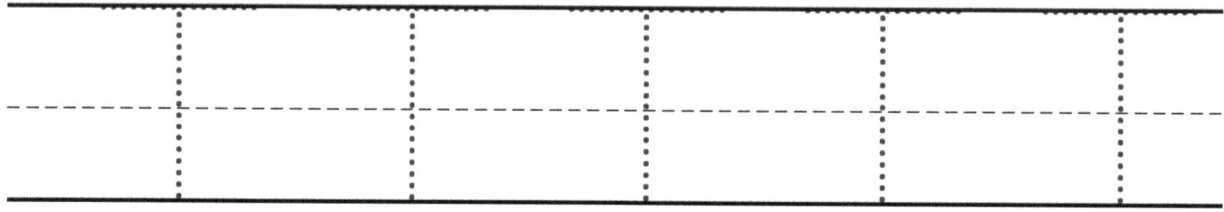

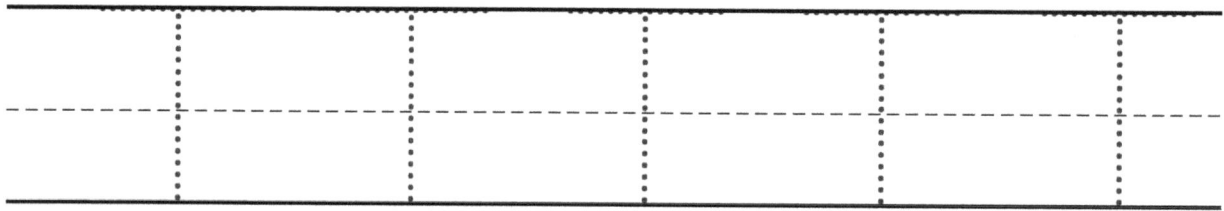

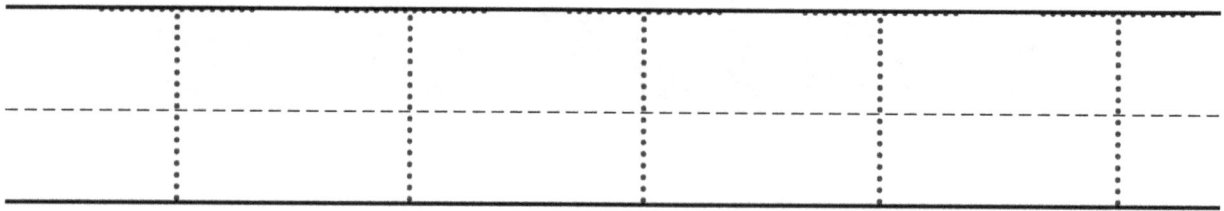

t t t t t t t t

t t t t t t t t

t t t t t t t t

t t t t t t t t

t t t t t t t t

t t t t t t t t

t t t t t t t t

Uu

Umbrella

U u

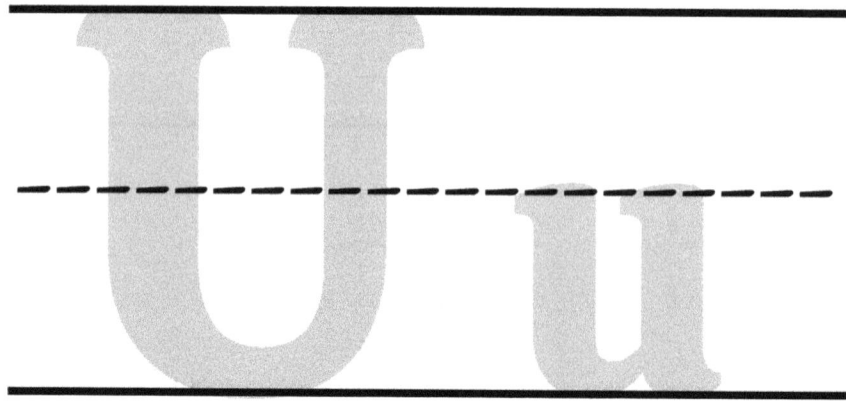

U is for Umbrella

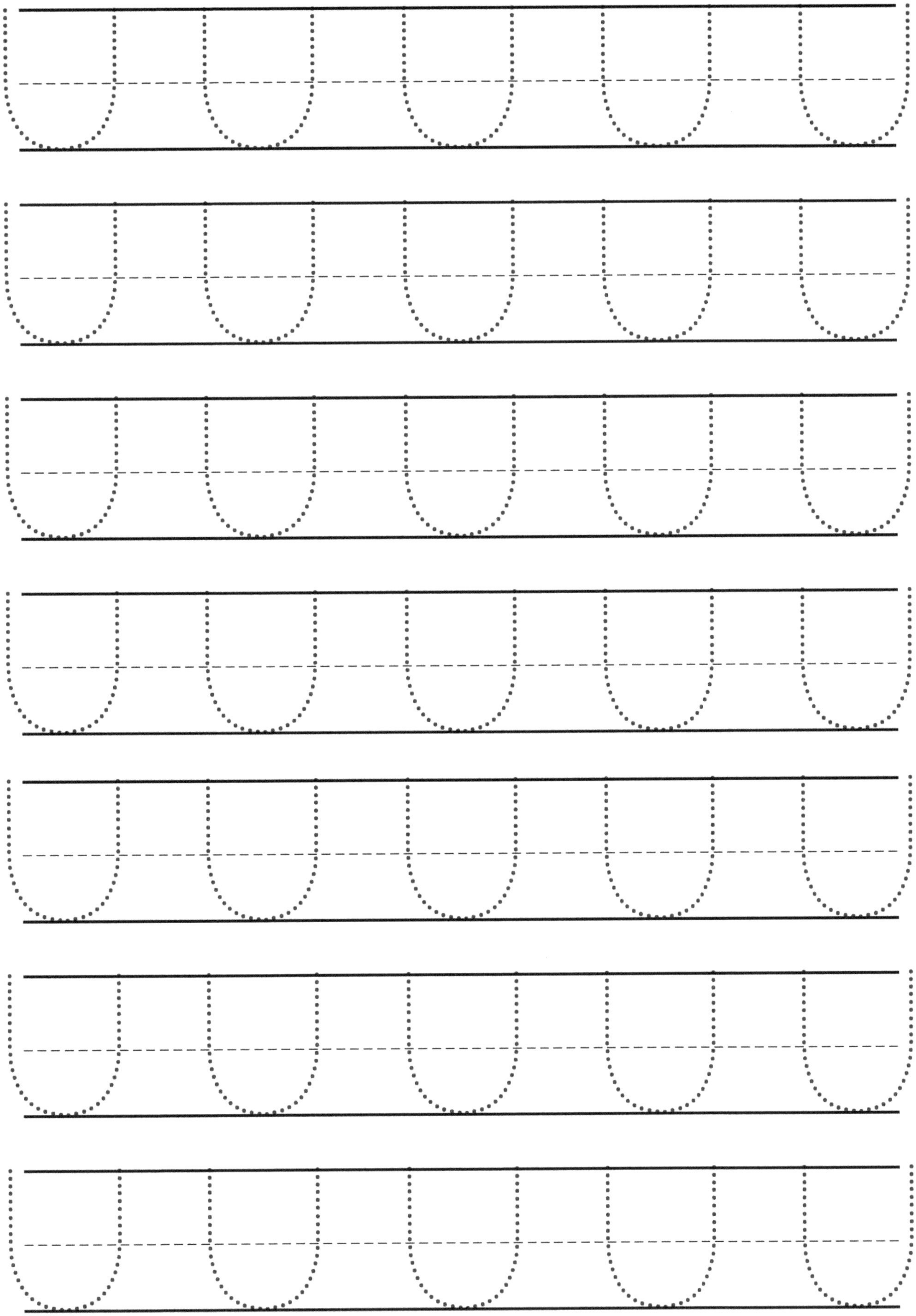

u u u u u u u u

u u u u u u u u

u u u u u u u u

u u u u u u u u

u u u u u u u u

u u u u u u u u

u u u u u u u u

u u u u u u u u

Vv

Volcano

V v

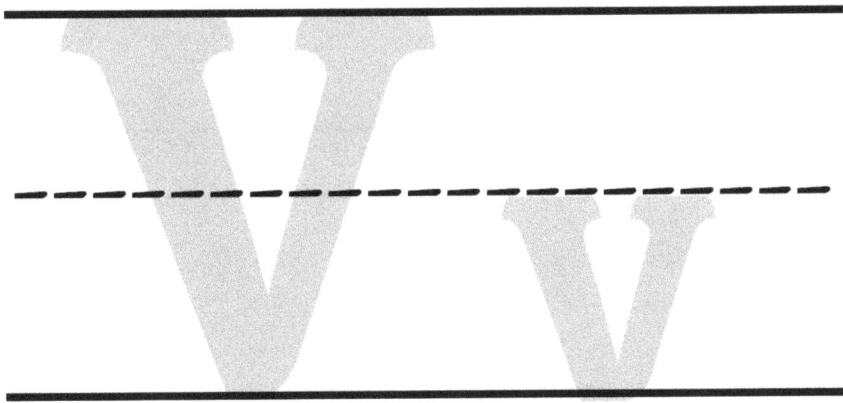

V is for Volcano

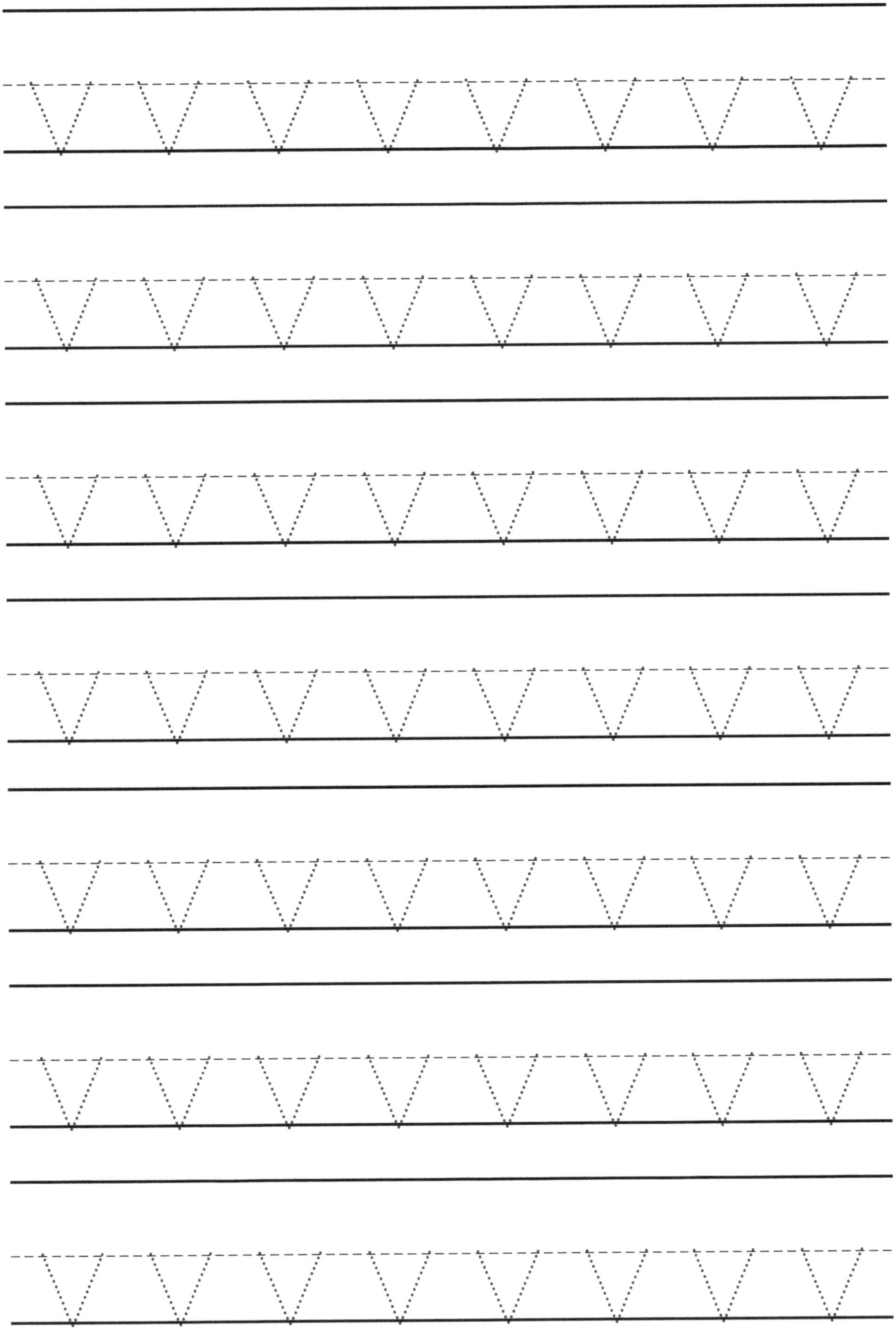

Ww

Watch

Ww

W is for Watch

w w w w w w

w w w w w w

w w w w w w

w w w w w w

w w w w w w

w w w w w w

w w w w w w

Xx

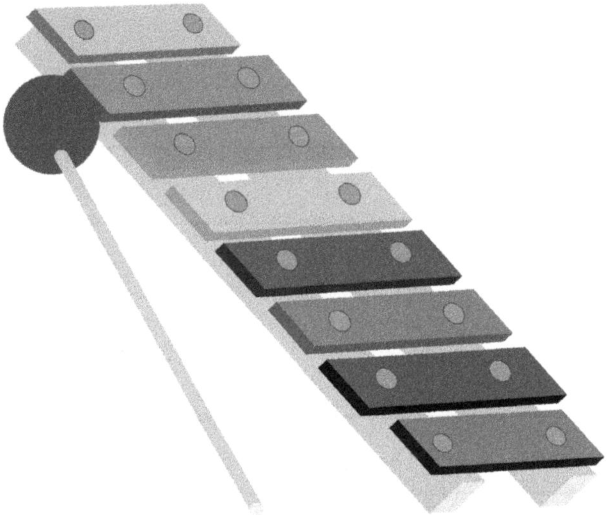

Xylophone

X x

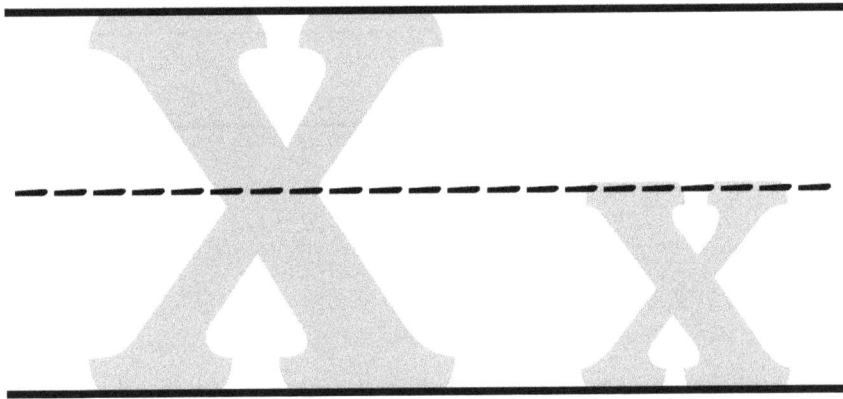

X is for Xylophone

X X X X X

X X X X X

X X X X X

X X X X X

X X X X X

X X X X X

X X X X X

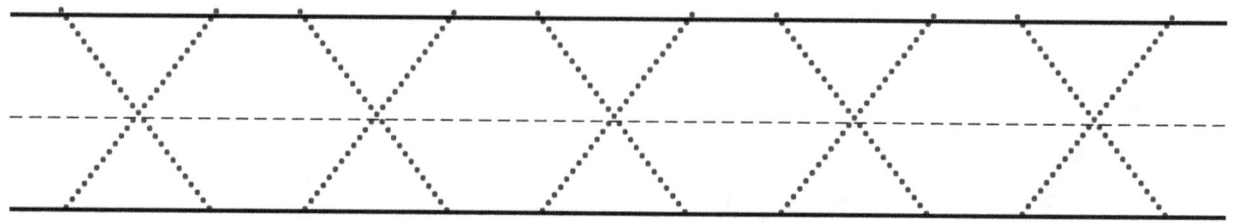

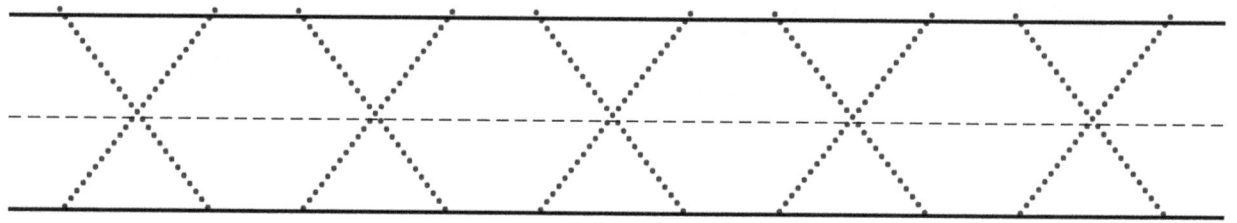

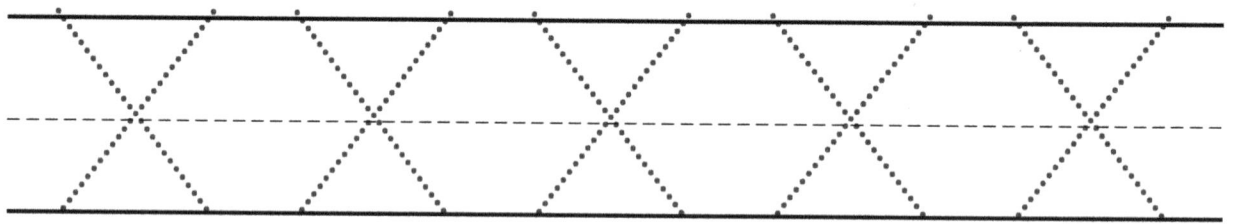

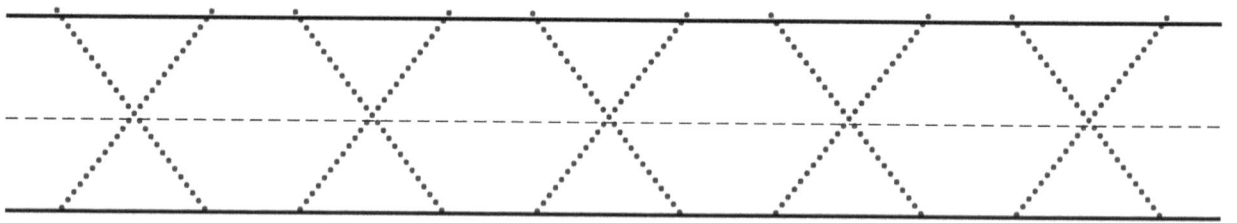

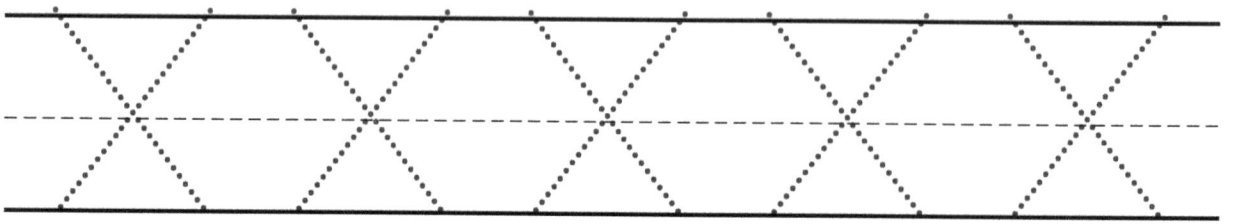

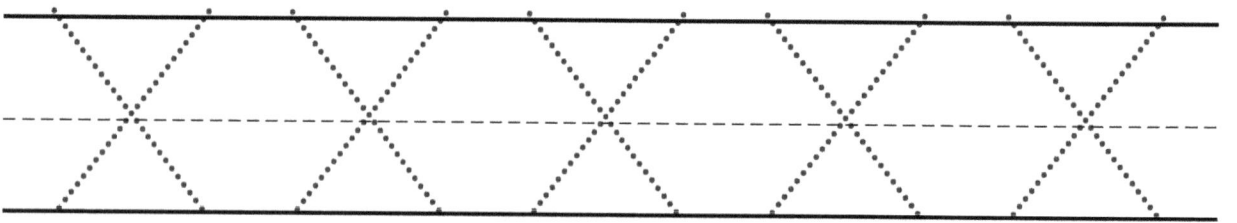

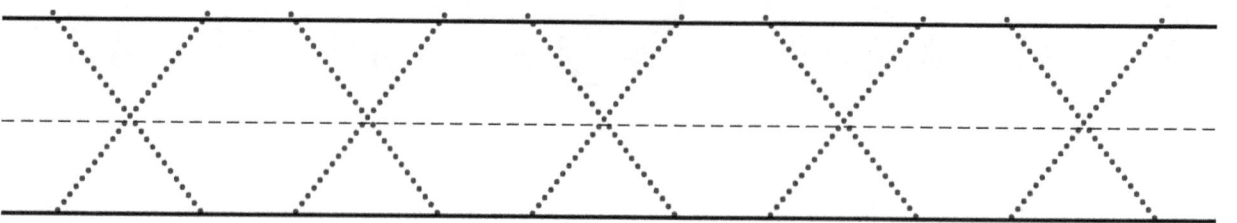

X X X X X X X X X

X X X X X X X X X

X X X X X X X X X

X X X X X X X X X

X X X X X X X X X

X X X X X X X X X

X X X X X X X X X

X X X X X X X X X

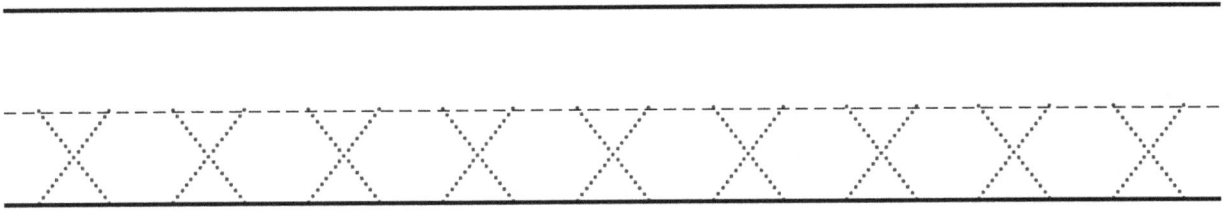

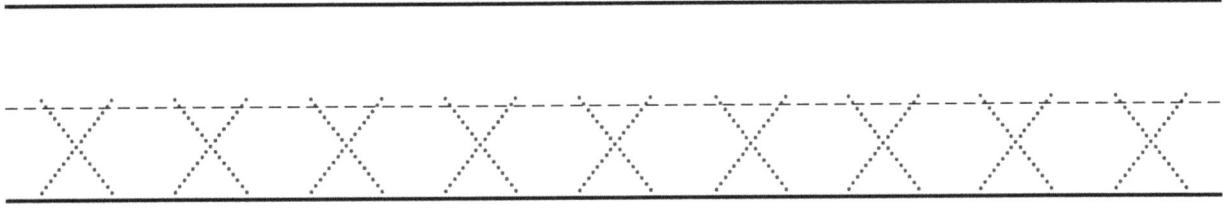

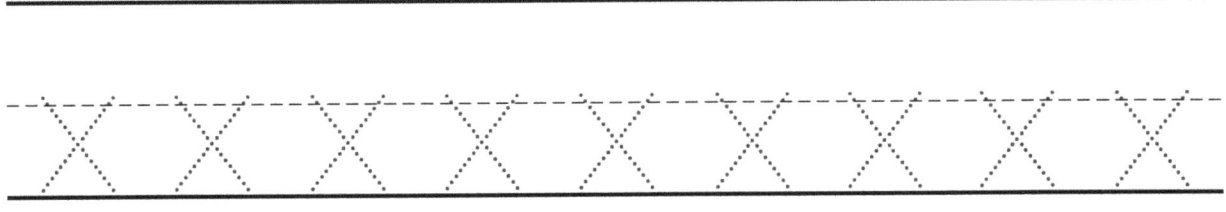

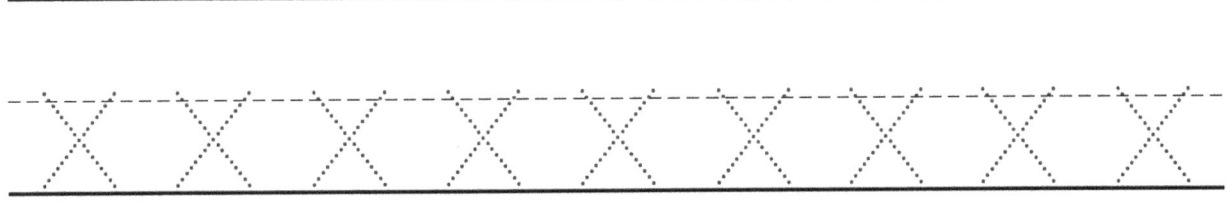

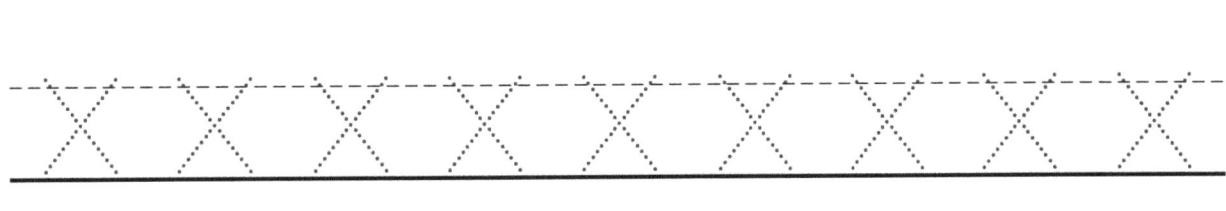

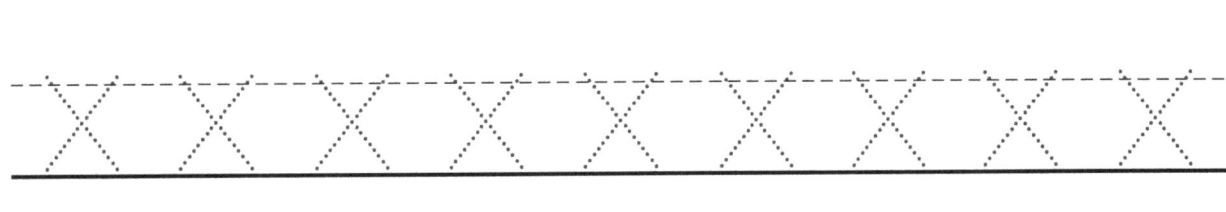

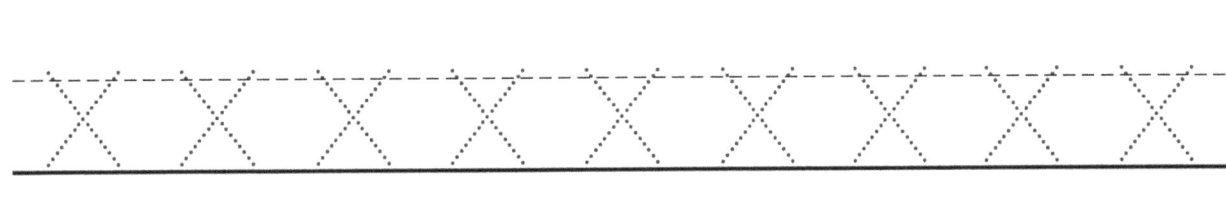

Yy

Yacht

Y y

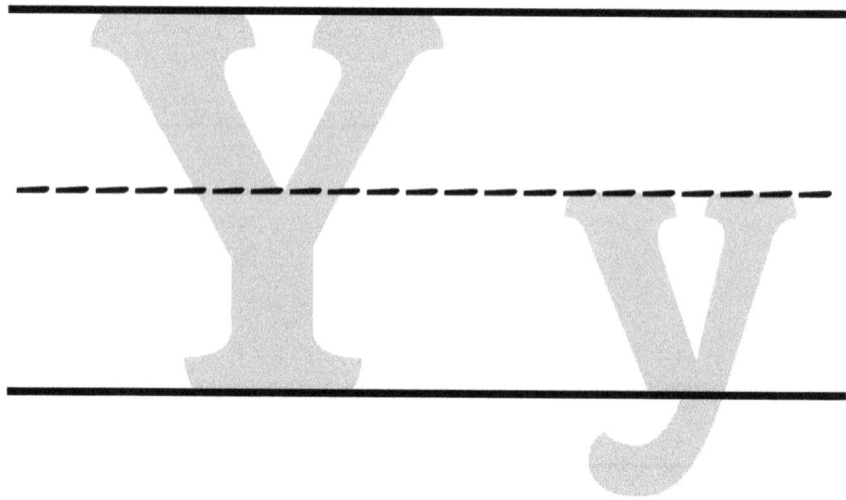

Y is for Yacht

Y Y Y Y Y

Y Y Y Y Y

Y Y Y Y Y

Y Y Y Y Y

Y Y Y Y Y

Y Y Y Y Y

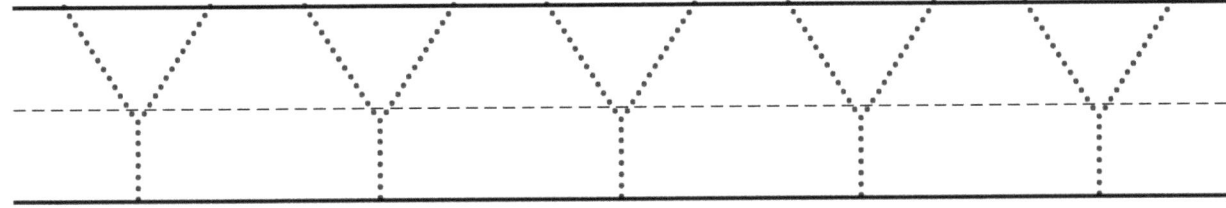

Y Y Y Y Y

y y y y y y y y

y y y y y y y y

y y y y y y y y

y y y y y y y y

y y y y y y y y

y y y y y y y y

y y y y y y y y

Zz

Zebra

Z z

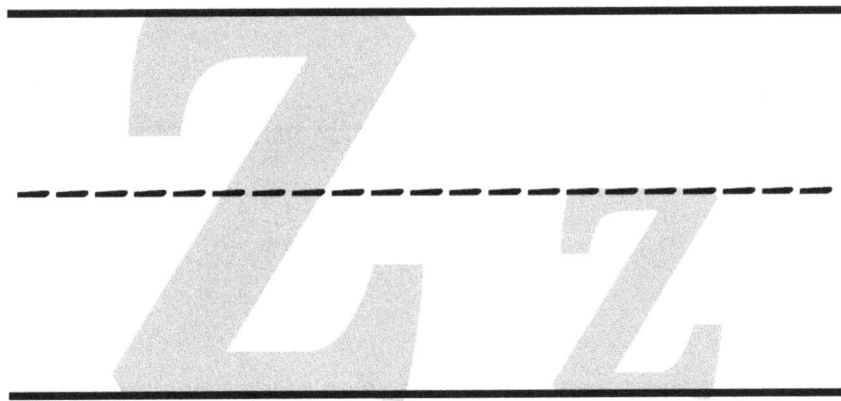

Z is for Zebra

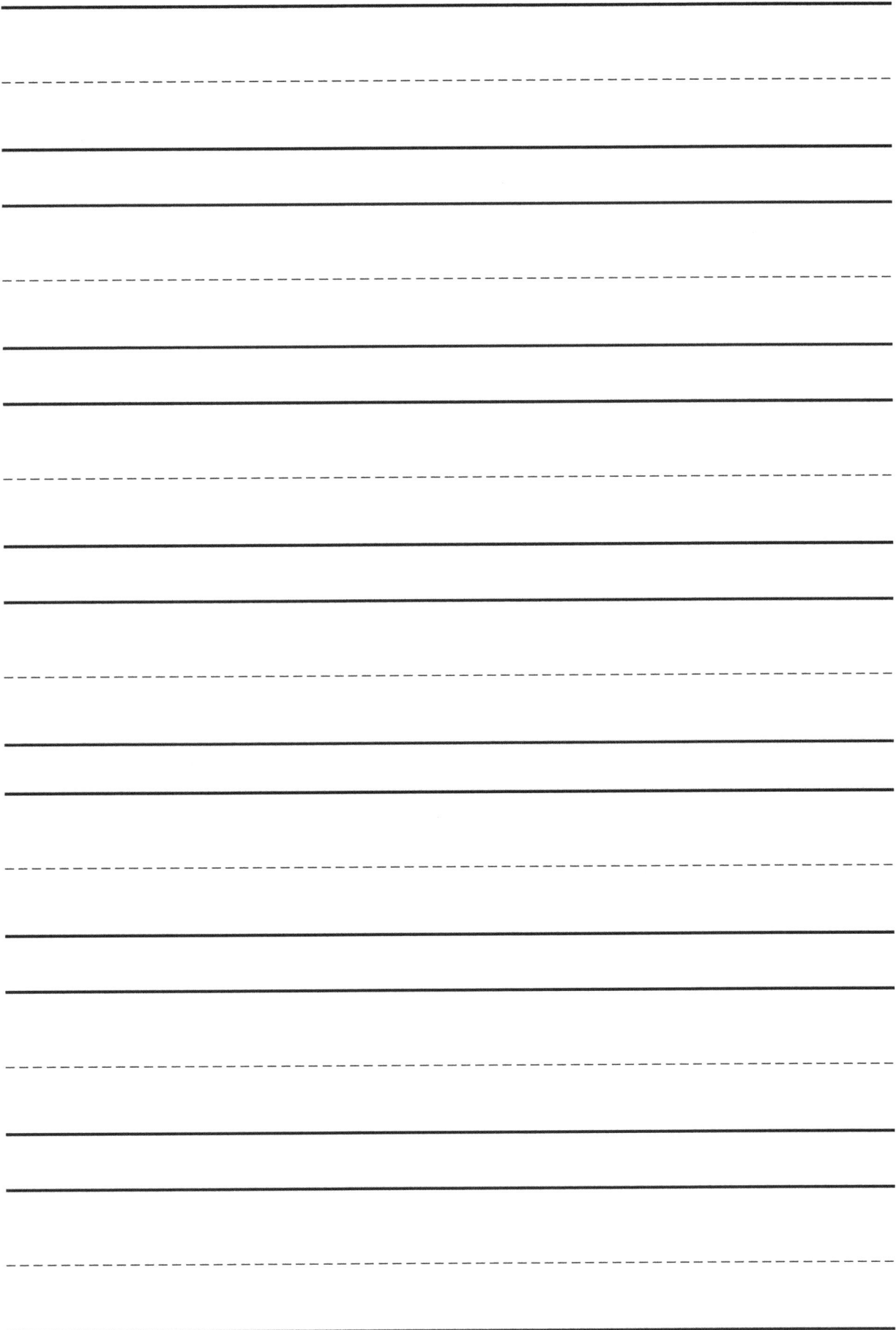

Lightning Source UK Ltd.
Milton Keynes UK
UKHW032155181220
375492UK00007B/169